STUDIES IN COLOSSIANS

The Savior's Supremacy

John L. Kachelman, Jr.

Copyright © 2021 Kachelman Publications.

All rights reserved. No part of this publication may be reproduced, stored in a retrieval system or transmitted in any form or by any means – electronic, mechanical, photocopy, recording, or any other – except for brief quotations, without prior permission of the publisher.

All scripture quotations, unless otherwise noted, are taken from the American Standard Bible (ASV).

Second edition. Revised and updated
First Printing 1985.

Published by Kachelman Publications
3918 Samantha Drive
Montgomery, Alabama 36109

http://www.kachelmanpublications.com

ADDITIONAL COPIES AND MATERIALS AVAILABLE ONLINE.

ISBN: 1-7326088-7-3
ISBN-13: 978-1-7326088-7-0

DEDICATION

To Guy N. Woods

whose life's labors as a scholar, preacher, and editor unite to illustrate the basic theme of this present study series, "The Savior's Supremacy!" He is one loved and respected and certainly faces a rich reward for his unwavering stand for the "old Jerusalem gospel." His influence has been felt throughout the brotherhood of Christ, and that influence will continue long after he departs to eternity's great reward. Those who know him know a man whose singular goal in life is to be well-pleasing to the Supreme Savior. May we all gain strength and courage from his devoted example and press onward toward the prize of the high calling of God in Christ Jesus.

John L. Kachelman, Jr.
St. Louis, Missouri
September 1985

TABLE OF CONTENTS

Materials for Teachers i

Forward iii

The Superiority of Christ v

The Dignity of Christ vi

1. Introduction to Colossians 1
2. The Supreme Savior Helps You to Accept (1:1-2) 11
3. Epaphras: A Man with a Supreme Savior (1:3-8) 23
4. Associates of the Supreme Savior (1:9-14) 37
5. The Savior's Supremacy (1:15-23) 51
6. Attitudes Instilled by the Supreme Savior (1:24-29) 63
7. Redesigned by the Supreme Savior (2:1-5) 77
8. Living Life with the Supreme Savior (2:6-15) 89
9. Supplanting Christ's Supremacy (2:16-23) 103
10. Branded by the Supreme Savior (3:1-4) 117
11. The Past Is Not Present with the Savior (3:5-11) 129
12. Supremacy's Visibility (3:12-17) 143
13. The Leaven of Christ's Supremacy (3:18 – 4:1) 157
14. Hankerings Fostered by the Supreme Savior (4:2-6) 175
15. A Chorus Sings Christ's Supremacy (4:7-18) 187
16. Short Sketches on Colossians 199

Materials for Teachers

Bible class materials were created and formatted for this series so a teacher can use them for presentation and discussion. These materials include handouts, and PowerPoint slideshows.

Your purchase of this book also entitles you to a free digital download of the lesson series materials from Kachelman Publications (use the code below for the free download at www.kachelmanpublications.com). This digital download includes a digital version of this book, individual lessons, handouts and PowerPoint slideshows for lessons. These materials should help you present the study and provide resources for teaching the series.

This free digital download includes permission to print the files as needed for use in the Bible class but does not allow the sale, transfer, copying, or dissemination of any kind of the digital files from the purchaser to any other user. The purchaser of this book has permission to make copies of the handouts for the class; however, this permission does not allow them to give an entire copy of the study to another person to use. An additional purchase of the digital download is required by other individuals other than the original purchaser. *Please note: if a congregation purchases these materials, they can be used multiple times for different classes in that congregation.*

CODE: SUPREME2021
ENTER CODE AFTER ADDING ITEM TO CART

FOREWORD

Paul's twin works of Ephesians and Colossians are mighty, marvelous and magnificent. The former is his magnificent masterpiece on the CHURCH of Christ; the latter is his marvelous masterpiece on the CHRIST of the church.

Worthy works dealing with Colossians among us are few and far in between. For this and other cogent reasons I am sincerely grateful for the powerful and painstaking work of John L. Kachelman, Jr., in Studies in Colossians: "The Savior's Supremacy." The title accurately describes the contents—serious studies in Colossians. Combined in this work are scholarship, practicality and deep devotion. Not often are all these so masterfully evident in a penned work, Brother Kachelman stays well with the text and sprinkles just enough illustrations through his work to shed helpful light on points discussed to give it balance in exegesis and applications of a current nature. He has given valuable background material that enhances the book of Colossians. His organization of material with the text stated and then explained, segment titles, drawing the material presented together in summary fashion and end-of-the-chapter reflections, questions, and resolutions makes for an easy and profitable perusal of this valuable work. He has an amazing vocabulary and makes masterful use of such in this literary production.

The entire book will be of great help to all Bible students in general and to preachers and Bible Class teachers in particular. The latter groups will find much value in the short sketches in the final section of the book. Nearly twenty pages are devoted to this type of study. They are "Seed for the Sower" relative to Colossians much like brother Leroy Brownlow's great work dealing with all parts of the Bible. They are great sermon or Bible Class starters.

It has been an enriching and profitable experience to read the manuscript. Brother Kachelman taught me many things about Colossians I did not know. He will do the same for you. It is a joy to commend this fine work.

Robert R. Taylor, Jr.
Ripley, Tennessee
September 16, 1985

THE SUPERIORITY OF CHRIST

A man had fallen into a deep, dark pit, and lay in its miry bottom groaning and utterly unable to move.

Confucius walked by and approached the edge of the pit, and said, "Poor fellow! I am sorry for you. Why were you such a fool as to get in here? Let me give you a piece of advice: If you get out, don't get in again."

A Buddhist priest came by next and said, "Poor fellow! I am very much pained to see you there. I think if you could scramble up two-thirds of the way, or even half, I could reach you and lift you up the rest." But the man in the pit was entirely helpless and unable to rise.

Next the Savior came by, and, hearing the cries, went to the very brink of the pit, stretched down and laid hold of the poor man, brought him up and said, "Go and sin no more!"

THE DIGNITY OF CHRIST

His very infancy not only startled a king, and made him fear his throne, but also affrighted the powers of darkness, and silenced the heathen oracles.

His childhood puzzled the knowledge of the aged, and confounded the doctors of the law.

He ruled the course of nature, and made the strong Winds obey him, and could walk upon the billows of the sea as if pavement.

He fed the multitudes by his word, and healed all manner of diseases without medicine.

He could command them to leap that were cripple, and make them to see the heavens and the day, who had been born blind.

He could cast demons out of their possessions, and restore the frantic to their wits.

He could break the gates of death, and open the doors of the grave and call back the spirits of the buried carcasses.

He sits exalted at the right hand of God, having led captivity captive and having removed the piercing sting of death and sin.

His is the name which alone saves the eternal soul, and which must ultimately be admitted by all of God's intelligent creation.

He patiently waits until time shall be no more and then he will appear, the shout of the arch-angel and the trump of God announcing his arrival. He will receive his blessed saints and escort them to Eternity's happy reward.

He alone is identified as "the Son of His love!"

─ 1 ─

Introduction To Colossians

I had just sat down to relax for a little time before enjoying a meal prepared by my wife, and the telephone rang bringing a message which I just cannot forget.

"Hello."

"Brother John, I hope that I am not interrupting your supper?"

"No, I was just waiting for it to get finished. How can I help you?"

"Well, this is ____, a new member at South Side, and I have a problem and I need to talk with you about it. My eighteen-year-old daughter is living in California. She is in a religious commune and wants to leave. There is one man who is the head of this group and claims to be directed by God in all decisions. This man has told my daughter that God does not want her to leave. Both she and I are very worried. I want to help, but I just do not know what to do!"

As we continued the conversation it was revealed that several other factors further complicated the situation. After the conversation, I sat back in amazement that someone would allow themselves to become ensnared in such a messy predicament.

It is extremely difficult to understand why some people will allow themselves to get so mixed up in life. The situation above is not an exception. There are hundreds of people close to us who share the same dilemma. They are confused, distressed, and bound by someone or something.

The book of Colossians addresses the problem of people being subjected to unreasonable and unscriptural controls. The one point which Paul stresses repeatedly in the Colossian letter is that we are bound to NO ONE or to NO THING because we are Christ's! We often ask, "Why do people allow themselves to be placed under the control of someone else?" Inspiration answers, "Because these people fail to give Christ the supreme position in life!" Our brethren in Colossae were on the verge of allowing themselves to be taken away from the supremacy of Christ and subjected to irrational designs of others. Paul's main emphasis in this epistle is to guide the Colossians into the knowledge that only Jesus Christ offers "completeness". Paul is careful to show that through Christ all things were created; and because of His uniqueness, Christ holds a position which should never be given to another. The answer to man's dilemmas, to man's surrender of his will to another, to man's passions with ritualism and mysticism, is found in the book of Colossians. That answer is a trust and confident faith in Jesus Christ.

As we begin a study of this rich book, it is useful to consider some basic introduction material. In considering these items we will find the message to be richer and add greater meaning to our modern lives.

AUTHOR & DATE OF BOOK

The Colossian letter was written by the Apostle Paul. Paul is referred to twice by name in the epistle (1:1; 4:18). The critics of the New Testament have generally agreed that Paul was the author of Colossians. The date of its composition is thought to be somewhere between 61-63 A.D. It was written while he was in prison (4:18). Because of his confinement, this epistle is classified as a "Prison Epistle" along with Ephesians, Philippians, and Philemon, which were also written at this time.

REASON FOR WRITING THE BOOK

As the epistle is read, it seems that Paul had three reasons for writing. *First*, Epaphras had arrived to visit with Paul and had brought Paul the news of the brethren's faith, love, and hope in the gospel (1:4, 5). This news stirred Paul to write these brethren, whom he had never met, and commend them for their faith and steadfastness (cf. 2:1-5). It does not require much imagination to see how greatly joyed Paul would have been upon receiving the good report on the church's welfare in Colossae.

Second, Paul had heard, most likely from Epaphras, about a menacing danger which threatened to pull the believers in Colossae away from their faithfulness. He wrote to counter the influence of this danger. This seems to be the major reason for writing (2:5, 8).

There may be a *third* reason. There might have been the need to let the brethren in Colossae know that Epaphras had arrived and that he was going to remain in Rome with Paul for some time (4:12, 13; Philemon 23).

ESTABLISHMENT OF THE CHURCH IN COLOSSAE

The establishment of the Lord's church in Colossae is not recorded in the New Testament. There seems to be two popular suggestions which attempt to educate silence on this point. Some suggest that the church was established while Paul labored for three years in Ephesus. At that time the Bible states that the entire area of Asia heard the gospel and was evangelized (Acts 19:10). That Paul did not personally establish the church in Colossae seems clear from the reference in 2:1. If Paul did not establish the church, it was probably established by those who worked closely with him. In this category we find two possibilities—Epaphras and Philemon. It may have been that these two men were converted by Paul in Ephesus and then went back to their hometown and established the church. That these two were influential figures in the church's life at Colossae is easily granted (Colossians 1:7; Philemon 1, 2, 17, 19).

There is a second possibility suggested. Those who were in Jerusalem and heard the first gospel sermon brought the message back home with them. There were those present from Asia (Acts 2:9). Colossae was known for having a substantial Jewish population and it is safe to assume that some of the Jews living there would have been present in Acts 2.

However, the church was established, the key fact for us to realize is that it was established. The brethren there grew in their faith, love, and hope following obedience. But when Paul wrote, there was the presence of error in the congregation. Error had been allowed to creep slowly in and if left unnoticed would have caused severe consequences for the brethren there. In fact, the life of the church was threatened.

GENERAL ATTITUDES OF COLOSSIAN CITIZENS

The citizens of this area were noted for their willingness to accept any new religious doctrine. Upon hearing a new idea, they would simply select what they liked the best and discard the rest. Whatever was liked would be added to the already existing religious practices. Their general attitude was "take and leave." To illustrate how widely this was practiced, history has preserved the account of a Jewish woman who was the honorary ruler of a synagogue and a priestess of the imperial pagan cult at the same time. These people were very adept at blending Jewish, pagan, and Christian ideas together and arriving at their own unique system of religion.

Another prevalent idea in Colossae was that the heavenly bodies (sun, moon, stars, etc.) influenced man's life on earth. They honestly believed that the stars had control over man. Added to this was the common belief that angels should be worshipped because of their influence on God. They felt that the angels were able to intercede for man and were capable of bringing about greater blessings.

Added to these two points, there was a philosophy which stressed intelligence as the way to arrive at "perfection." It was taught that in order for a person to arrive at perfection, or to arrive at a state of harmony with God, advancement had to be made through the intellect. They taught that man was able to rise above this world's limitations and enjoy the life of the gods IF he could arrive at a perfect knowledge.

Thus, these three points—blending or religious ideas, superstition, and trusting one's intellect—combined to present a philosophy that was threatening the very existence of the Lord's church in Colossae. When we understand this, we can well understand why Paul stresses to his readers, "*Seek the things above, where Christ is, seated at the right hand of God. Set your minds on the things that are above, not on the things that are upon the earth*" (Colossians 3:1-4). The brethren at Colossae had to understand that only "in Christ" was it possible to find "perfection."

THE COLOSSIAN HERESY FURTHER DETAILED

From Paul's writings to the Colossians, we are able to distinguish several points which comprise the dangerous threat.

It foreshadowed the Gnostic heresy of the second century. Although this error was not fully developed until the second century, it is found in early stages in the first century. This philosophy stressed "knowledge" (i.e., from the Greek GNOSIS — "to know") as the way to arrive at perfection. The Gnostics taught that all matter was evil and that only the spirit was good. They denied that God created the universe and that Jesus came in the flesh. (To see Paul's clear rebuttal to these two points, carefully read Colossians 1:16-22.) The result of this philosophy was one of two things: (1) Living a life that was totally immersed in sin. They reasoned: since flesh is evil, nothing our physical bodies do can be held against us. (2) Living a life that was devoted to severe treatment of the body. They reasoned: since flesh is evil, let us make sure that it is constantly punished.

The Gnostic philosophy was dangerous for a number of reasons; but perhaps the greatest threat to our Colossian brethren was the promise of a spiritual union with God *IF* they attained perfect knowledge. Thus, they could be united with God by some means other than Jesus Christ.

It included the legalism of Judaism. Emphasis was laid on the observance of days and seasons, religious regulations and forms that had been bound by the Law (2:8-11, 16, 17).

It included mysticism. It claimed that the truly "knowing ones" were capable of receiving visions and revelations (2:18). It included the worshipping of angels and the heavenly stars (1:16; 2:10, 15, 18).

It de-emphasized Christ by asserting that He was divine BUT there were other things just as essential for salvation. They were willing to provide Christ with a place in religion; but they were unwilling that this place be the one of supremacy (1:18; 2:9).

HOW USEFUL IS COLOSSIANS TO MODERN MAN?

We can readily see the significance of Paul writing to the brethren at Colossae to instruct them about the tragedy which was coming upon them. But how does all of this apply to those of us living in this modern age? Is this epistle, written to an ancient town, about an ancient heresy, still important?

One of the characteristics of inspiration is its perennial youthfulness. This is seen in Colossians. The writings in this epistle, though addressed to people living centuries in the past, are just as necessary today as then. The relevancy of these inspired instructions is seen as we consider the four challenges to Christ in Colossae and the answer of inspiration to each of these four.

Our brethren faced *the challenge of Gnosticism*. They were being confronted with a philosophy which, if followed, would result in dire consequences. This same challenge confronts believers today. We are constantly being challenged with PHILOSOPHY. The secular world boasts of certain theories and philosophies which undermine the fundamental gospel truths. If we yield to these philosophical challenges we will stand just as Colossae, deceived by philosophy.

Our brethren faced *the challenge of Judaism*. There were those who desired to bind hard requirements, manners of dress, and diet. Today believers face a similar challenge in LEGALISM. There are still those who spurn the free grace of God and instead of living in the liberty of God's grace, they encourage others to place themselves under bondage to a system or a person.

Our brethren faced *the challenge of mysticism*. They were told that a subjective [emotional] basis was the sole authority in religion. Today we face those who trust in MYSTICISM to decide religious matters. We are told that visions are still possible and that God uses these to direct our ways. We are warned to follow the stars, and there are many around us who have their "charts" read so that they can make a decision about life!

Our brethren faced *the challenge of the world*. They were told to seek this world's wisdom as the means of finding perfection. We are also encumbered with the ever-present threat of falling prey to the allurements of the WORLD and trusting the world instead of God for life's purposes.

These four challenges—philosophy, legalism, emotionalism, and materialism—still plague believers in our modern era. They may not parade around in the garb of first century dress, but they are still with us! Unless we are careful, we will fall prey to their evil designs. This is where we see the wonderful relevance of the book of Colossians. It seems as if Paul was anticipating our needs and writes as though he sees the trials and troubles believers face in life today. The book of Colossians is useful because it addresses the challenges of life!

Several years ago, two nice-looking, young men rang my doorbell. They introduced themselves as "elders" and wanted to come in and study the Bible with me. I invited them in and as we sat down to study the Bible, they told me that they had something in addition to the Bible. The addition, they claimed, would make the Bible "more perfect." They proceeded to tell me about a "modern prophet" who lived in the 1800s who had received prophecy from a certain angel. I was told that I could be "saved" by following the Bible, but if I wanted to be "exalted" I must follow their "latter-day prophet". These two were sincere and honest in their convictions, yet they failed to realize the message of Colossians. *WE DO NOT NEED ANYTHING ELSE BUT THAT WHICH HAS BEEN SUPPLIED BY JESUS CHRIST!*

FOR FURTHER PREPARATION TO STUDY COLOSSIANS

1. Read the entire book carefully several times and list the positions which Jesus Christ holds.

2. Research the city of Colossae in an encyclopedia or dictionary and offer additional remarks on its area and customs.

3. Look carefully at the four challenges to Christ's supremacy that are addressed in Colossians. How are these challenges to modern Christians?

4. How does astrology pose a threat to Christ's supremacy? Look in several different publications and see what the modern attitude toward astrology

is. Check your concordance and see what other references can be found which speak of astrology. What is God's attitude toward astrology?

5. Why do you think Paul stressed the supremacy of Christ in light of all the problems which the Colossian brethren had? How would this help their situation?

6. Carefully formulate a study outline on Colossians using the theme "The Savior's Supremacy!"

═ 2 ═
THE SUPREME SAVIOR HELPS YOU TO ACCEPT LIFE

"Paul, an apostle of Christ Jesus through the will of God and Timothy our brother, to the saints and faithful brethren in Christ that are at Colossae: Grace to you and peace from God our Father."
(Colossians 1:1-2)

Little Annie came out of her Bible class with a smile spread across her tiny face, her eyes sparkling. She seemed as though she was unable to bear some pleasure that rested deep within her. When asked, "Annie, why are you so happy today?" she replied, "Oh, I have just found out how much God loves me! God's love forgives me when I am bad and He wants ME to live with Him forever and ever!" Such joy found in a little, innocent child is a delight to behold. The great Apostle to the Gentiles shared this joy in his life. In our present text we find Paul in a Roman prison, chained to a member of the elite pretorian guard twenty-four hours a day. He was not afforded any privacy, for wherever he went the guard followed. His conversations were always listened to by the guards. Yet the epistles written during this time are filled with joy, hope, contentment, and a confident trust in Almighty God!

Why is it that Paul possessed this inner joy in the face of such trying situations? What enabled him to live with such a contented and confident trust in God's will? The answer is found in his understanding of the Savior's Supremacy. Of all the major characters in the New Testament, Paul stands out as the one whose life emphasizes the Savior's Supremacy the most. Here we see one who placed himself under the Savior's control. His own words often reveal this submission, *"I have been crucified with Christ; and it is no longer I that live, but Christ liveth in me: and that life which I now live in the flesh I live in faith, the faith which is in the Son of God, who loved me, and gave himself up for me"* (Galatians 2:20). I am sure that no one could have been in the presence of Paul very long and not have become aware of WHO his Lord and Master was. It was because of this belief and conviction in Christ Jesus as the Supreme Savior that Paul could look at the events of life with joy-filled expectation.

Our present passage is commonly signified the "salutation" of the Colossian epistle. Paul is dictating this letter, probably to Timothy, and the opening verses follow the customary style of his time. However, because of the Savior's tremendous influence on his life, even these opening words contain a vital message for present day readers. Within these verses we are able to discover four realizations of Paul which caused him to possess joy and contentment in life. By a simple application of these truths to our lives we should be able to experience the same joy today. Look carefully and discover why Paul was able to accept life with joyful trust!

PAUL COULD ACCEPT LIFE BECAUSE HE REALIZED...
THE WONDERFUL PROVIDENCE OF GOD

"By the will of God" (1:1)

Paul looked around. Where he was, what he was, and who he was were all attributable to the providential working of God. He was shackled; he was in prison; his fate was to be determined by a pagan court; yet, he looked at the whole situation as appointed by God! In Philippians (also written while he was in this Roman jail) Paul affirmed that he was *"set for the defense of the gospel"* (1:16). When comparing other thoughts of translating this expression, it is interesting to notice that the idea is suggested that he had been "appointed" or "placed there for" that purpose. The word for "set" is from the Greek KEIMAI and when this word is used in the New Testament of persons, it means "to be specially set, solemnly appointed, destined" (Thayer's, *Greek-English Lexicon*, p. 343). Paul looked at his present situation as an opportunity afforded him by the providential working of God! He had been placed in that Roman jail for the defense of the gospel, and he was going to make sure that the message progressed. Here we discover a man who held an unshakable trust in the providential working of God. In the Philippian epistle, Paul remarks, *"The things which happened unto me have fallen out rather unto the progress of the gospel...I know that this shall turn out to my salvation...For it is God who worketh in you both to will and work, for his good pleasure"* (Philippians 1:12, 19; 2:13). Because Paul realized the supremacy of Christ, he was able to be confident even in the most anxious moments of life. He could honestly state, *"We KNOW that to them that love God all things work together for good, even to them that are called according to his purpose"* (Romans 8:28).

Because he realized the providential working of God, Paul did not think of himself as a criminal in prison hopelessly awaiting an uncertain fate. He knew that he was a messenger of Christ! He knew that he was chosen by the will of God to be there. Because of his realization, Paul looked at himself as *"an apostle of Christ Jesus through the will of God"*. He was saved because the providential will of God had made known the plan of redemption. He was an apostle sent to the Gentiles because the providential will of God had so chosen and afforded him opportunity to accept such a position. Paul was able to view the providence of God as the means of his salvation, the source of his strength, and the secret of his success. Even a casual reading of Paul's letters will reveal his dependence upon the providence of God. For example, in Romans 15:23 Paul states, *"That I may come unto you in joy through the will of God..."* Paul was addressing the saints in Rome. He was intending to visit with them (Romans 1:11-13). It is significant for our study to note that Paul intended to go to Rome but it would be "through" the will of God. When he wrote Colossians he was in Rome, not as he intended; but it was still "through the will of God" that he was there! Carefully read the following texts and observe how frequently Paul confesses his total dependence upon the providential will of God—Acts 18:21; Romans 1:10; 1 Corinthians 1:1; 4:19; 2 Corinthians 1:1; Galatians 1:4; Ephesians 1:1, 2.

Paul realized that the will of God was strong enough to answer any difficulty of life. He could confidently trust that no matter what happened to him in life, things would eventually work out for his best interests because he followed the Supreme Savior. Such a confident trust is often hard to demonstrate when life's pressures are intense.

A man once visited one of the great museums desiring to see a tapestry that was well known. As the man stood before the hanging, he could not make sense of the scene. He knew it was to depict a town scene with men, horses, and roads; but to him it seemed a continued nonsense. There was neither head nor foot and it seemed a total confusion of threads and colors. But then it occurred to him that he was looking at it from the wrong side. As he stepped around to look at the tapestry from the proper perspective, what formerly was confused and meaningless became exact proportions. Such is often true with the providential working of God. If we look at them with mere reason divorced from faith and trust, we will find nothing but nonsense, muddle, and disorder. But if we look from the proper perspective, we find that all events fit in exact proportion. Then a beautiful history will unfold clearly depicting the care and consideration of the Almighty One above! Confident trust is available only to those who, like Paul, have found the secret of the Savior's supremacy in their lives.

PAUL COULD ACCEPT LIFE BECAUSE HE REALIZED...
THE BELIEVERS' POSITIONS IN LIFE!

"Saints," "Faithful brethren," *"In Christ" (1:1)*

These words were deliberately used by Paul to show his readers the wonderful positions which are available to those who obey the Supreme Savior. Notice the positions which are available.

One is a "SAINT" of God. It is unfortunate that this beautiful term has become so corrupted in our day. A "saint" in the New Testament sense was not a person who was elevated to that position because of some excellent performance. Whenever Paul and the other New Testament writers spoke of a "saint", they did not have in mind a figurine that adorns the dash of an automobile or a small corner of a garden. The "saint" of the New Testament was a person who was "set aside for God's use" (cf. 1 Corinthians 1:2). The concept of holiness is found in the word "saint." In the Old Testament we read of a number of items which were "holy" unto God. There were places (Exodus 29:31) that were "holy." There were people who were "holy" (Leviticus 20:7). There were things that were "holy" (Exodus 28:2). Thus, the idea of being a "saint" or of being "holy" is that the thing, person, or place is set aside for the use of God alone. An excellent character comes as a consequence of being set aside for the sole use of the Lord God.

Another position that results when we place Christ in a supreme position is that we become a part of the "FAITHFUL BRETHREN." The word "faithful" suggests the idea of honesty and a desire to perform according to a proper standard. Paul knew the importance of encouraging his readers to remain "faithful" because they were saints.

The third phrase which describes the believer's position is a comprehensive one — "IN CHRIST". This is a common phrase of Paul's. In fact, in the book of Colossians alone we discover its presence about twenty times! To Paul this phrase was the best way he knew to express the relationship and union of the believer with Christ Jesus. So important was this concept to Paul that Christ actually became his life, and the daily life he lived was governed by the will of Christ (cf. Galatians 2:20). To Paul this was a grand blessing. Although he was in Rome and those who were to receive this epistle were hundreds of miles away, each found a common location for they were all "in

Christ!" This beautiful position can never be taken away from those who truly seek to serve and obey God.

From these three positions we are able to discover some most impressive teachings.

First, those who are in these positions will make the insignificant the most significant! In looking at the city of Colossae, the following points are noted. It was a small and insignificant town. With the passing of years its importance dwindled and it became of no significance. Its larger and more prosperous neighbors would soon overshadow it and help in the demise of its standing. But this small, insignificant town is remembered today solely because of the people there who shared in these three positions! Such is certainly true today. Look at yourself. Are you important? Are you significant? As the world judges you, the answer may be "No." But as God judges, the answer is "Certainly! You are most significant!" Your value is determined by the position you hold in relation to God. If you possess these three positions, you are extremely valuable.

Second, those who occupy these three positions are duty bound to add strength to one another. We are faithful brethren who are in Christ. This denotes a tenderness, unity, and togetherness. You cannot be "in Christ" and go off to live in solitude! God designed His church in such a way that togetherness is essential if we are going to be acceptable saints and faithful brethren. Paul realized this and that is why he is writing the Colossians. He wanted to add his strength to theirs and by this help them remain faithful and firm.

Third, those who hold these positions are bound to accept the obligations which these positions possess. As a saint we must seek to live our lives properly because we have been set aside for God's use alone. We must be pure and consecrated. As brethren we must recognize the blessed family tie which binds us together. As brethren we must remain "faithful," following carefully the will and instruction of our Lord. As those who are "in Christ," we must make sure that Christ is the center and source of life each day.

Then there is a wonderful thought that comprises our *fourth* point. Since we are "in Christ," we share a security which cannot be matched. It really does not matter where we are or what befalls us because WE ARE IN CHRIST! As the old hymn expresses, we are "safe in the arms of Jesus."

PAUL COULD ACCEPT LIFE BECAUSE HE REALIZED...
THE FAR SURPASSING BLESSINGS OF THE SUPREME SAVIOR

"Grace and peace"

Although these words were commonly used in the greetings of that time period, the Apostle expresses them with added meaning. The Colossians had accepted the wonderful GRACE of God. They had heard the gospel message presented by Epaphras and had obeyed it (cf. Colossians 2:10-12). In their obedience they came in contact with the marvelous favor which God bestows upon all who obey His will. After the grace was accepted, PEACE was bestowed. The Colossians were once again "bound together" with God because sin had been washed away in their obedience and that which had separated them from God was thus removed.

These two blessings are available only to those who own Christ as the Supreme Savior. Only as we look to Christ can we find means by which the grace of God can be accepted and our sins forgiven. It is only after our sins have been forgiven that we are able to find blessed peace--the quiet and tranquil calm which overcomes anxiety, tension, and frustration.

PAUL COULD ACCEPT LIFE BECAUSE HE REALIZED...
THE WARM, FILIAL RELATIONSHIPS ENJOYED BY THOSE WHO FOLLOW THE SUPREME SAVIOR

"Brother," "Brethren," and "our Father"

There is discovered a wonderful and warm relationship with others of like faith. Inspiration tells us, *"For ye are all sons of God, through faith, in Christ Jesus"* (Galatians 3:26). And again, *"Whether one member suffereth, all the members suffer with it"* (1 Corinthians 12:26). Imagine the membership at Colossae. There you would find master and slave, rich and poor, men and women, Jews and Gentiles; but Paul says they are all "brethren." Here is a beautiful picture. Despite the differences in culture, social status, and opinions, they were brethren.

There is a story told of a pious man of high social standing who was in the habit of associating with pious people of low social rank, even those so low in society that they were considered "outcasts." One day a worldly friend confronted him about this association and expressed surprise that such would be publicly shown. The noble Christian man replied with a sentiment befitting only one who understands the beauty of a common brotherhood in the Lord. He remarked, "I can hardly hope to enjoy the elevated ranks as a redeemed saint of God in heaven with these brethren if I should spurn the association with them in the present!" How true was his remark!

The brotherhood shares a love which must be demonstrated. It we allow the petty prejudices and opinions of this world to disrupt our association now, how can we be granted association in heaven? If you feel hesitant or unable to associate with a fellow-saint here on earth, it will be impossible for those feelings to get you into heaven. Whenever we realize the beauty and blessing of such relationships, it will contribute to a glorious unity in the Lord's body. Then there is discovered a warm, tender relationship with God above. No longer is He some mysterious "god" who is far removed and unconcerned about our lives; but now He becomes "OUR FATHER." What a beautiful thought. We have the privilege of calling Him our Father because we have become His children.

DRAWING IT ALL TOGETHER

Paul was able to sit in a Roman jail, chained to a guard, and be as happy as if he were walking around a free man. This ability to rejoice was due solely to the fact that he recognized Christ Jesus as the Supreme Savior. Paul knew that he had obeyed his Savior's will and was therefore "in Christ" where safety was assured. He knew that his heavenly Father's will would be carried out regardless of the trials and tragedies life threw before him. He knew that he shared a warm and tender relationship with his "brethren in the Lord." Because Paul knew these things, it really did not matter to him what the world did or said. Paul had the secret of a source of strong support which assisted him to overcome all trials.

This beautiful peace of mind can be yours today. The key to it is found in these four realizations of Paul. If the Savior is supreme in your life, then you will share in these realizations.

REFLECTIONS & RESOLUTIONS

Reflections from our study of Colossians 1:1, 2:

1. *Reflect* once again on the joy-filled life of the Apostle Paul. What were the four points suggested in our lesson which could account for his joyful attitudes? Which is most important to you? Why?

2. Reflect the wonderful providence of God. Search and record other Bible passages that discuss this providence or reveal God's providence in His dealings with man. What are three things about the providence of God that give comfort to you?

3. Reflect on the phrase "in Christ." How does this describe present-day believers? Do you think that Christians seriously contemplate this position in their lives? If all believers would look seriously at being "in Christ," would this change their lifestyles? Think about the blessed security that is offered to those "in Christ." How long is this security to last? What will threaten this security? How does 1 John 1:6-10 confirm the security of the child of God?

Resolutions arising from our study of Colossians 1:1, 2:

1. Resolve that you will develop the same confident trust which Paul shared in the providential will of God. Decide that your prayers will reflect a desire for the Lord's will to be done.

2. Resolve that you will appreciate and deepen the positions you are privileged to hold as God's child.

3. Resolve that you will deepen the relationship that you share with your brethren and your Father in heaven.

— 3 —
EPAPHRAS: A MAN WITH A SUPREME SAVIOR

"We give thanks to God the Father of our Lord Jesus Christ, praying always for you, having heard of your faith in Christ Jesus, and of the love which ye have toward all the saints, because of the hope which is laid up for you in the heavens, whereof ye heard before in the word of truth of the gospel...bearing fruit and increasing, as it doth in you also, since the day ye heard and knew the grace of God in truth; even as ye learned of Epaphras our bellowed fellow-servant, who is a faithful minister of Christ on our behalf, who also declared unto us your love in the Spirit."
(Colossians 1:3-8)

An interesting story is told which serves to highlight the need for constant dependence upon God. During the Battle of Lake Erie, when in the sweeping havoc which was sometimes made, a number of men were shot away from a gun emplacement. Those surviving looked around silently to Commander Perry, and then stepped into place of their fallen friends. When the Commander looked upon those who lay wounded upon the deck, he always found their faces turned towards him and their eyes constantly fixed upon his countenance. The presence of trial and danger did not cause their gaze to lessen.

As we open our Bibles to the present text, we discover a man who was a soldier in the Lord's army. Here we see one whose gaze never left his Supreme Commander! Through these verses we are properly introduced to Epaphras, the first century gospel preacher. Throughout this section, the personality of this minister is dominant. Paul's words speak of the recognition of a warm friend. From the text, and others which mention Epaphras (Colossians 4:12, 13; Philemon 23), we are able to detail the following about this man. He was responsible for the Colossians' understanding of the grace of God. He was a member of the Colossian church, a citizen of Colossae. He was a faithful minister of Christ Jesus and a bond-servant to his Lord. He labored much for his brethren in Colossae and in Laodicea and Hierapolis.

Epaphras is a shortened form of the name "Epaphroditus," but he is not the same one referred to in Philippians (2:25: 4:18). We know very little about this man. There are some who have given interesting observations about him, but these are not founded on fact, just fiction. For the sake of curiosity, I mention the following about him. [Note that the following is not based upon fact, just supposition.] Some assume that he was a business man who taught and preached in Colossae. It is further supposed that he became a Christian while in Ephesus on a business trip. Following his conversion, he eagerly returned to Colossae to preach Christ. He later went to Rome on business and while there visited the Apostle Paul. Tradition has suggested that this man became the first bishop of Colossae and the first martyr in that city. It is far more likely to view Epaphras as a preacher of the gospel who labored with the saints in Colossae and had journeyed to Rome to seek Paul's counsel on the heresy that was threatening the church in Colossae.

Whatever the past history of Epaphras may be, we are certain of the facts that are expressed by Paul in the Colossian letter. From this short paragraph, we are able to see a wonderful picture of a minister of Christ who was deeply devoted to His Lord and Savior. Here is one, as those sailors on Lake Erie, who never took his eyes off of the Supreme Commander!

From the present text, we are able to see just how the supremacy of Christ affected Epaphras in two vital areas. *First*, we will discover how the Savior's supremacy directed Epaphras in his teaching. *Second*, we will discover how the Savior's supremacy affected Epaphras in developing personal relationships among his fellowmen and with God and Christ Jesus.

WE DISCOVER HOW THE SUPREME SAVIOR GUIDED EPAPHRAS IN HIS TEACHINGS OF CHRIST JESUS (1:3-6)

The diligence of this first century preacher is readily seen in the content of his teaching. What does one teach who knows that Christ is the Supreme Savior? Epaphras answers this question for us. Consider the following thoughts carefully.

First, Epaphras taught the triune graces of Christianity—faith, hope and love. The combination of these three graces was no accident. These three are often combined in the New Testament and stand as a capsule summary of Christianity (see 1 Corinthians 13:13; Romans 5:1-5; Galatians 5:5, 6; Ephesians 4:2-5; 1 Thessalonians 1:3; 1 Peter 1:3-8; Hebrews 6:10-12). Whenever Christ is supreme, these three graces will be prominent in the teachings. Consider each one in brief detail.

FAITH is the source of belief and conviction for the child of God. In fact, it is the only way in which the child of God will find proper directions. Paul affirms that we "*walk by faith, not by sight*" (2 Corinthians 5:7). This "faith" is not just mere intellectual "belief" but it is an intense action that is initiated by understanding that God has spoken to man and expects a response in return. This desire, which stems from faith, is founded as one opens the revealed will of God and finds the Lord's will for man. "*So belief cometh of hearing, and hearing by the word of Christ*" (Romans 10:17).

It is this "faith" which provides the atmosphere for the child of God to live in; for faith enables one to find the way to be "in Christ" (Galatians 3:26, 27). It is this "faith" that is the root of the Christian's life and, in fact, becomes life for the believer (Galatians 2:20). Thus, when Epaphras taught the Colossians about "faith," he was teaching them about the entire system upon which Christians stand accepted in God's sight. Much more was taught and commanded by this first century preacher than mere "believing (intellectual assent) on Christ!" This faith which the Colossians demonstrated was a beautiful confidence in the ability of God's provisions.

It is best illustrated by a small child. What is the tiny tot able to do? If turned out on its own, it would quickly become lost. And if left alone, it would soon die of want. He cannot find the next meal or furnish his own shelter. And yet, what fear or concerns does the small child have about these needs? Does he show concern or alarm? Not in the slightest! The reason why is that here is one who, in a beautiful manner, lives the life of faith. That small child who cannot purchase the next loaf of bread has a firm conviction that his "daddy" can. Even though he is unable to provide the clothes necessary for tomorrow, he has an unbounded confidence that "momma" can do so. Even though the small child cannot provide for even the most basic needs, he does not share a moment's concern. Here then is a beautiful and simple explanation of a perfect life of *faith*.

Now our brethren in Colossae share a life of faith similar to this. The faith was shown in their lives because a preacher was careful to instruct them about *faith*.

LOVE is a quality which results from mature understanding. As the believer matures in the Christian faith, there is an equal maturing in this quality of the heavenly Father. John tells us that we have the capacity to love, and to develop this love to the greatest degree because God has first loved us and has shown us the example (1 John 4:19). This love will be demonstrated in our speech, attitudes, and daily conduct. Paul said that this love of Christ "constrained" him (2 Corinthians 5:14); it propelled him in daily life. This love will seek the general welfare of all men, but especially it seeks out those who are members of the "household of faith" (Galatians 6:10). To try to limit or restrict this love is to place barriers which God never intended His followers to erect. As Epaphras taught the brethren in Colossae, he was careful to instruct them about this great love which must demonstrate practical Christianity.

Then there is the marvelous HOPE which Epaphras proclaimed. Hope is a great blessing to the believer. This implies much more than a "wishful outlook" on the future. Hope to the child of God is a confident expectation. This marvelous hope is "living" (1 Peter 1:3ff); it is able to "purify those who possess it (1 John 3:3); and it is able to strengthen believers in anticipation of the Lord's blessed return (1 John 2:28).

Carefully consider that Paul stressed this "hope" had been "laid up" (Colossians 1:5), or "reserved" This word is used in regard to money that had been deposited into one's account. It is reserved for that one person. Thus, this blessed hope is the possession of the believer alone. This hope should give believers strong assurance in the face of trials and struggles. Obstacles in this life should never move us away from this blessed hope. When properly used in the believer's life, this hope serves as an anchor both "sure and steadfast" (cf. Hebrews 6:19).

In 1683 Vienna was besieged by the Turks, and the Emperor of Austria had to flee the city. The citizens of Vienna sent to the King of Poland for aid. They knew in which direction the Poles would come, and watched the way long and anxiously. At last, they saw the lances of their rescuers gleaming on the mountain trails leading to Vienna. That very day their foes were defeated and their city was set free. In like manner, hope enables the Christian to look expectantly with a calm assurance for the Lord's return. Each believer, because of this hope, should be *"looking for the blessed hope and the appearing of the glory of our great God and our Savior, Jesus Christ"* (Titus 2:13).

As Epaphras taught this hope to the believers in Colossae, three things were certain to result. This hope would have assured them of the good things that were to come. This hope would have prepared them for the reception of these good things. And this hope would have enabled them to await patiently the arrival of these good things.

Second, Epaphras taught the word "of truth," the gospel message (v. 6b). This was in contrast to those who were then teaching error in Colossae. Notice that Paul is careful to state that the "word of truth" is what they had heard "before." They did not need any "new" teachings. They needed to follow the old teachings which had been preached earlier. This seems to indicate that there were those in Colossae who were listening to the false teacher's philosophy that "old" is of no value. God always exhorts His followers to stay a steady course on His revealed will. It is Satan who is the "Author of change" in doctrine. Even in the Old Testament God urged His followers to look carefully and see where the "old paths" were. When these old paths had been found, they were to be quick to following them. But unfortunately, just as in Colossae and even in our time, there were those who refused to walk in the "old paths" (cf. Jeremiah 6:16, 17). We too must be reminded that we should follow the "original gospel" message. To add to it or delete from it will prove eternally injurious! It will be a point of broad approval by God for His preachers to stand before Him and receive the commendation that they, just as Epaphras, had taught and preached so that their listeners had heard "the word of the truth of the gospel."

Third, Epaphras taught God's grace clearly. So plain and simple was the preaching of Epaphras that his audience "knew" [understood] the grace of God. Perhaps this is the best compliment that could be given to this first century preacher. His lessons were so plain that those who heard went away with a full understanding.

Spurgeon tells of a small town in the Hartz mountains called Goslar. In this town there was a fountain in the square. It was peculiar in that no one was able to reach the water so as to be able to fill a bucket, or even get a drink to quench his thirst. Both the jets and the basin were above the reach of ordinary men; yet the fountain was placed there to supply the town with water! The purpose of the fountain was totally missed. Such results when one who preaches the gospel fails to make the wisdom of God understood to those who listen.

There are a few observations which must be made about this "grace" of God which Epaphras preached. It should be noted that Epaphras taught this grace "in truth." In order for the grace of God to be understood, it must be taught "truthfully." There are many today who teach about the grace of God but they fail to teach it "truthfully." It should also be pointed out that when understood, the grace of God will free people from the bondage of man's doctrines and legalism. God's grace introduces us to the freedom shared by all who are in Christ. If the Colossians would pause and remember the blessings of God's grace, they would never place themselves under the bondage of legalism. It should also be pointed out how intimately Christ, salvation, and the grace of God are connected. If one is forsaken, then the other two must be forsaken as well. You cannot have God's grace without obeying Christ; and you cannot have salvation without God's grace and obedience to Christ. These three are inseparable.

Epaphras taught these three things [the triune graces of Christianity; the gospel; grace] as he labored with the Colossian believers. Taken together they serve well to outline the ministry and blessing of Christ. Only as one has Christ as the Supreme Savior will he be able to preach and teach as Epaphras did in Colossae.

Because of his diligence in teaching these three things, Epaphras was rewarded. There was "thanksgiving." Paul was thankful because the Colossians had received the gospel message. There was "constant prayer." Not only was Paul praying for the Colossians, but also the believers in Rome were praying. There was "fruit bearing." The message of the Supreme Savior carries with it a life-giving power. The blessed fruits (cf. Galatians 5:22ff) will be clearly evident in the lives of those who listen and obey the Lord's will.

WE DISCOVER HOW THE SUPREME SAVIOR GUIDED EPAPHRAS IN
DEVELOPING PROPER RELATIONSHIPS (1:7, 8)

Carefully notice how Epaphras was directed in developing the proper *relationship with his fellowmen.* Because he acknowledged Christ as his Supreme Savior, he recognized that he was to be a "servant." He understood that his Savior expected him to offer service to others. Christ had commanded, "I have given you an example, that ye should do as I have done to you . . . A servant is not greater than his lord . . . If ye know these things, blessed are you if ye do them (John 13:15-17). Epaphras was willing to follow the steps of Christ and serve others. He was willing to be used so that others could find happiness and joy.

I remember a stream with an old mill on the shore. The mill's wheel had turned constantly for year, never breaking down, never moaning, just the same steady service. The brook which turned the mill flowed in the same steady manner. Every place that its waters went there was growth and beauty and life. These two servants [the mill wheel and the stream] well illustrate the service of Epaphras. It was constant, never ceasing, and everyone whose life was touched by this service was encouraged to grow and develop. It was because he became a servant to others that three wonderful things could be said about Epaphras.

First, he was "beloved." There was a warm affection which was stirred when the memory of his work was brought up. Wouldn't it be wonderful if the thoughts of each reader stirred this same affectionate emotion? *Second*, he loved to talk about others (cf. Colossians 1:4, 8). I like this point about Epaphras! Epaphras informed Paul about the Colossians. Here is a man who loved to talk about others in a positive and upbeat way. What a blessed friend this type of person is. One of the greatest compliments in the Bible is paid to Job when Eliphaz said, "Behold, you have admonished many, and you have strengthened weak hands. Yours words have helped the tottering to stand, and you have strengthened feeble knees" (Job 4:3, 4). I believe that Job and Epaphras could stand in the same company as men who knew how to use their tongues. *Third*, he labored earnestly for others in prayer (4:12). What a marvelous comment! He was so concerned about the spiritual welfare of his brethren that his prayers were intense and "laboring." If we could instill this type of prayer habit in our lives, just imagine the great progress which Christ's cause would experience.

Epaphras could develop this intense and intimate relationship with his fellow brethren because of his relationship with God and Christ (v. 7b). He worked in submission to his Lord. "Minister" means one who works "under" another. Epaphras wanted nothing but to be faithful and loyal in serving his Savior. He wanted to help the Lord, as the Lord directed!

DRAWING IT ALL TOGETHER!

From the life of an obscure preacher in the first century we are able to see how allegiance to Christ as the Supreme Savior will richly bless our lives.

There will be blessings as we teach the wonderful gospel of Jesus Christ. We will be sure that we are teaching only the "truth." We will be sure to teach the vitals of the gospel—faith, love, and hope. We will carefully consider our teaching so that the grace of God will be clearly understood, that all who hear us will want to put aside legalism and man's doctrines and find the true freedom that is "in Christ."

There will be blessings in our personal relationships. As we hold the supremacy of Christ foremost, we will follow our Lord's example of serving. From this life of serving Christ, we will become "beloved" workers who anxiously speak about others in an uplifting manner. We will be concerned about the spiritual well-being of others to the extent that we will "earnestly labor" for them in our private devotions with God. As we recognize Christ as the Supreme Savior, we will recognize our submission to His will. We will become "ministers" who are honest and loyal to our Savior's commands.

One closing observation must be made. Although Epaphras held the supremacy of Christ and this fact is revealed in his teaching and in his relationships, the brethren at Colossae PERSONALLY had to accept inspiration's counsel and fully obey *before* Christ could become their Supreme Savior. We must not base our salvation upon someone else's relationship with God. Our parents may fear God and obey God, but their obedience does not save our souls. My marriage partner may serve God faithfully, but his/her obedience does not justify me from my sins. It is a personal decision. Carefully study verses 4, 6, and 7 to see how the Colossians personally applied the gospel's message to their lives. This obligation is bound upon each reader today. The gospel has come to YOU! What will YOU do with its commands? YOU cannot own Christ as the Supreme Savior until YOU have fully submitted to His will in YOUR life! This personal duty cannot be avoided. Follow Epaphras' example and obey God's will completely in your life this very day.

REFLECTIONS & RESOLUTIONS

Reflections from our study of Colossians 1:3-8:

1. Reflect on the various virtues which Epaphras possessed. Which do you think is the most important? Why? Is this one you have seen in believers?

2. Reflect on Epaphras' ability to teach the Colossians the grace of God. What allowed him to teach this grace so clearly? Why has the "grace of God" become so confused in our time? What can be done to help people understand God's grace better?

3. Why are the three graces (faith, love, and hope) so vital to the believer? Take a concordance and find other passages which discuss each of these graces. Write a definition of each one in your own words.

4. Reflect on the necessity of believers becoming "servants." Turn to John 13:1-35 and record the actions and attitudes which God's servants must possess.

Resolutions arising from our study of Colossians 1:3-8:

1. Resolve that you will become as Epaphras in your teaching and in developing relationships. Realize the need to put "self" aside and follow Christ completely (cf. Luke 9:23).

2. Resolve that you will develop your teaching talents so that you may be able to present the

gospel in plain and simple language so that those who listen to you will understand fully.

3. Resolve that you will act so that others will look upon you as a "beloved" servant who builds others up with speech and labors and who earnestly expresses concern for the welfare of the brethren.

— 4 —
ASSOCIATES OF THE SUPREME SAVIOR

"For this cause we also, since the day we heard it, do not cease to pray and make request for you, that ye may be filled with the knowledge of his will in all spiritual wisdom and understanding, to walk worthily of the Lord unto all pleasing, bearing fruit in every good work, and increasing in the knowledge of God; strengthened with all power, according to the might of his glory, unto all patience and longsuffering with joy; giving thanks unto the Father, who made us meet to be partakers of the inheritance of the saints in light; who delivered us out of the power of darkness, and translated us into the kingdom of the Son of his love; in whom we have redemption, the forgiveness of our sins."
(Colossians 1:9-14)

One of the most impressive traits of the early Christians was their effect upon the non-believers. Our first and second century brethren were the objects of ridicule, insult, and multiplied tragedies; yet, amazingly enough, the secular historians speak of their behavior in glowing terms. One of these historians, Tertullian, observed, "The heathen are wont to exclaim with wonder, 'See how these Christians love one another!'" What was it that caused the first century believers to be recognized in this way? It was association with the Supreme Savior!

There is an old Latin proverb which states, "If you are always walking with those who are lame, you will yourself learn to limp." This proverb speaks of the importance of one's associates influencing and compelling his actions. Many are like the tiny tree frog. This unique creature acquires the color of whatever it adheres to for a short time. If it is found on an oak, it is a brownish color; on the sycamore or cedar, it is a whitish-brown color; but, when found on the growing corn, it is sure to be green. Just as the association of the tree frog determines its color, this principle of association is verified in matters of the spiritual realm. In Exodus 34:29-35 we read that the continued association of Moses with Almighty God caused a definite effect on his person. In the book of Acts, the first century brethren were known because of their association with Jesus Christ. "They took knowledge of them, that they had been with Jesus" (Acts 4:13b).

In our present passage, the careful student is able to see this principle of association demonstrated once again. Paul has greeted his brethren and is about to begin the main body of the epistle. As he begins, he reveals an intimate fact—he has been praying for his brethren on a regular basis! From this passage we are able to see the prayer requests of Paul clearly outlined. From this prayer we will find a pattern that all believers would do well to imitate. Yet, if we limit our thoughts to the prayer of Paul in this text, we will greatly restrict our understanding of this passage. There is within these verses a wonderful lesson which stresses how constant association with Christ, as the Supreme Savior, will be seen in daily living. Clearly revealed to us is the fact that IF we associate with Christ, we will demonstrate this association in life. We will be as the brethren in Acts 4, for when others look at us, they will take "knowledge" that we have been with Jesus. Do you want that commendation? Of course, you do! In order to deserve it, you must demonstrate your association with the Supreme Savior in the following four ways.

THOSE WHO ASSOCIATE WITH THE SUPREME SAVIOR DEMONSTRATE...
A STEADFAST DEVOTION AND CONCERN FOR OTHERS (1:9)

This devotion will be demonstrated in our prayers. We will constantly practice the mention of others as we pray to God. Look at how often Paul has stressed his prayer habits for those whom he had never met: "praying always" (v. 3); "do not cease to pray" (v. 9). I like the comment that another has made about these expressions of Paul. He suggested that they were an "affectionate hyperbole." Paul was a person who deeply felt his brotherly affection—even for those brethren he had never met. The American Standard Version reads "we also" in verse 9. This rendering suggests that Paul had been praying for the Colossians and the Colossians had ALSO been praying for Paul. Here then we discover a beautiful picture of the devoted affection which is shared by those who have the same Supreme Savior. Once we are able to see the supremacy of Christ Jesus, then we will be able to develop an accepting and forgiving spirit toward fellow men that is exactly like the Lord's (cf. Romans 15:7; Colossians 3:12, 13). It is hard to imagine a way of demonstrating your devotion for another that does not include this tender and constant praying for their best interests.

This devotion will also be demonstrated in our desires for the advancement and maturity of others spiritually. It may be easy to "mouth" a prayer for someone else, but you can never offer a shallow prayer for another if you are truly interested in their spiritual development. The expression "That ye may be filled" suggests that Paul was deeply concerned about the development of the Colossians' faith. The word "filled" is interesting to consider. It can be understood in any of three ways: [1] It can refer to the Colossians being "fully equipped." The word is used to describe vessels that were made ready for a long voyage. These ships were equipped to face the dangers and challenges which awaited them during the journey. If understood in this manner, Paul desires that the Colossians possess everything that they need to journey through life in a safe way (cf. Colossians 2:10). [2] It can refer to being "fully controlled by knowledge." When we are "filled" with knowledge, we are controlled by it. In Ephesians 5:18 Paul speaks about our being "filled with the Spirit." He is talking about our being directed and controlled by the Spirit's teachings (found in the Scriptures). Understood in this manner, Paul's prayer is that the Colossians would be controlled by a knowledge of God's will. [3] It can refer to "advanced maturity." Whenever we are "filled with the knowledge," all imperfections are removed. Understood in this manner the Apostle's request is that the Colossians grow to maturity so that all imperfections are eliminated and the deepest understand and practice of God's will be found. Any of these three meanings could well suit Paul's intention. He was anxious that his brethren be "filled" so that they would be equipped to travel through life safely; he desired that they would be fully controlled by God's will and that they would press on toward full maturity.

It is important to see in what direction our concern and devotion for brethren is to be directed— "the knowledge of his will in all spiritual wisdom and understanding." We should be concerned that our brethren be "filled" with God's wisdom and understanding of His will. This phrase tells us "how" the filling is to take place. It also tells us "what" should govern our prayers. Both should be regulated by the "will of God." There are some who are confused today on how God reveals His will to modern man. Some suggest that "feelings" are how we can know God's will. These say, "I know that God is leading me in this direction because I just *feel* that it is right." Others wait for some divine revelation, for a "voice speaking from nowhere." Others have become hostage to events and situations in life claiming that "God doesn't want me to do this because so-and-so happened." As Paul wrote to the Colossians, there did not exist this confusion. Paul simply stated that they would be "filled" as a result of knowing God's divine will. A simple investigation of verses 3-8 will provide us with a clear discussion on how the Colossians received knowledge of God's will for their lives. They heard the gospel preached (v. 5). As the gospel was preached, God's will was made known. Thus, in order for modern man to know what the will of God is, he must read and study the Bible*! It is in the Bible alone that God's will is going to be found today.* (Notice: If there is any dispute about this point, the good reader is referred to the following texts for closer study: Ephesians 3:1-5—God's will has been revealed by His inspired preachers and teachers; Jude 3b—God's will has been "once for all delivered." As a newborn cannot be delivered but once, the will of God has been "once for all delivered"; 2 Timothy 3:16,17—through the work of inspiration, all that we need to teach, reprove, correct, and instruct has been furnished.) As we govern our prayers by the revealed will of God, we will be praying the proper things. As we are "filled" according to the will of God, we will develop the proper "wisdom" and "understanding" of spiritual matters.

Do you share this devotion and concern for others? Only those who are "associates of the Supreme Savior" will demonstrate this!

THOSE WHO ASSOCIATE WITH THE SUPREME SAVIOR DEMONSTRATE...
A DESIRE OF SERVING GOD'S WILL (1:10, 11)

Here we discover a very crucial fact. When we associate with the Savior, we will develop an intense desire to be "pleasing" unto Him. This word, "pleasing," is often used to describe the service of a slave toward a master. The slave will do anything to cause his master to be pleased with his service. The servant will try to anticipate the master's wishes. As the concept bears on our relationship with Christ, we discover that our association with Him will result in our doing anything that is commanded and even trying to "go beyond" that which we think is normal duty

This desire is illustrated by two biblical characters—Paul and Enoch. Paul states his desire in 2 Corinthians 5:9, "*We make it our aim, whether at home or absent, to be well-pleasing until him.*" Enoch is forever remembered as the man "who walked with God." But have you ever considered why Enoch walked with God? Hebrews 11:5 gives us the answer, "*by faith Enoch was translated that he should not see death, and he was not found, because God translated him: for he hath had witness borne to him that before his translation he had been well-pleasing unto God.*" Enoch tells us that the desire to be well-pleasing must be demonstrated! You cannot have this desire without demonstration and be acceptable to God. YOU MUST

"WALK WITH GOD!" In the lives of these two Bible characters, we discover a desire and the demonstration of this desire.

As Paul writes to the Colossians, he mentions this desire and demonstration. They were to be "well-pleasing" unto God; but how can the desire be demonstrated? Paul tells us that it should be shown in four simple ways.

First, our desire is demonstrated by "walking worthily." This refers to one's daily lifestyle. It causes us to recall Philippians 1:27— "Only let your manner of life be worthy of the gospel of Christ." There Paul refers to the conduct of citizens. Because we are citizens of heaven, let us conduct ourselves as such! I like the expression which Moody used, "Every Bible should be bound in shoe leather."

Second, our desire is demonstrated by "bearing fruit." The scriptures are very plain in teaching the necessity of "good works" [fruits] to salvation. One simply cannot be saved and not perform good works (cf. James 2:20; 2 Corinthians 5:10.

Third, our desire will be demonstrated by an "increasing with regard to the knowledge of God." This is the maturing process which is a consequence of following the will of God in our lives. Our desire to please God will prod us to study and understand His wonderful revelation [The Bible] and through this study we will mature (2 Peter 3:18; 1 Peter 2:1-3).

Fourth, our desire will be demonstrated as we are "strengthened with power." We will remain strong because our strength comes from God; it is according to His might, not ours! We have the power to do whatever we must do to obey His will. Notice that Paul tells us how this power source will affect our lives.

We will have power to be steadfast! This refers to our remaining true to God when we are faced by trying events and circumstances. When we are faced with life's trials, we can draw upon God's power and strength to see us through. The Hebrews were encouraged to remain true to God by looking at that great "cloud of witnesses" and run in a steadfast manner the race that was set before them (Hebrews 12:1). Those disciples in Acts 2:42 remained steadfast in the face of opposition because they had access to the divine power source which enabled them to overcome. If you are easily overtaken by the trials of life, look carefully at your association with the Supreme Savior. The proper association will stimulate a desire to please Him and this desire will provide the necessary strength to remain steadfast.

We will have power to be longsuffering. This refers to our ability to tolerate and forebear irritating people in life. Have you ever been insulted or personally wronged and felt that you just had to react in a similar way? If not, you are a very unique person! Paul tells us that we have the means available so that even when we are deeply hurt by insults and wrongs, we can remain calm and collected. You do not have to "blow your stack." You are associated with the Supreme Savior and this enables you to be strong! Whenever you are confronted with that person who aggravates you, remember your association and the power you have because of it.

We will have power to be joyful. The Christian is the only person in this world who has the right to joy! We, alone, have the power available to meet all difficulties with a joyful trust and confidence in God. This requires a strength which God alone can offer. This joy is the fruit of the Spirit in the believer's life (Galatians 5:22ff). This does not mean that you will laugh in the face of trials and ills and tragedies; but it means you will possess a self-contentment knowing that whatever befalls you God is in charge and His will is going to be done! Because God's will is going to continue uninterrupted, you rejoice. The Apostle, as he sat in the very jail from where he penned this letter to the Colossians, remarked, "*I rejoice, yea, and will rejoice. For I know that this shall turn out to my salvation*" (Philippians 1:18b, 19). His power gave him strength to rejoice. If you do not have the strength to rejoice at life's ills, look at your association with the Supreme Savior. Is it proper? Has it become severed? Has it been neglected?

THOSE WHO ASSOCIATE WITH THE SUPREME SAVIOR DEMONSTRATE...
AN ABOUNDING THANKSGIVING FOR GOD'S GOODNESS (1:12, 13)

Whenever Paul's name is mentioned, I am sure that there are many associations immediately made. But two of the most common will be his prayers and his thankfulness. Here we see his thanksgiving for three things which God did for the Colossian believers.

Paul was thankful because God had "qualified" the believers. He had "made them meet" to be saved. This qualification was essential so that the believers would be competent to wear the title of "God's saints." How did God do this? What all was involved in this? The Colossians had been in the world, lost in sin, captives in the snare of Satan. In order to become a saint of God, they had to escape the captivity of Satan and find the freedom of Christ. Thus, whenever we find out what they did to escape sin and become a part of Christ, we will discover what they had to do to be "qualified." The Bible is clear in telling us what must be done.

First, one must "hear" the gospel of Christ preached so that his heart will be opened to the truth (Romans 10:14ff; Colossians 1:5-7; Acts 16:14ff). *Second*, after the sinner has become aware of his lost state, he earnestly seeks to know what he must do in order to be rescued by the blood of Christ (Acts 2:37; 22:10a). *Third*, as one desires redemption and earnestly seeks to discover God's will, he further studies the Bible. In further study it is discovered that "repentance" must be shown (Acts 11:18; Luke 13:3).

Following repentance is the desire to "confess" the Son of God. God's book has instructed us as to what must be confessed (Matthew 16:16; Acts 8:37), and why this confession is essential (Matthew 10:32, 33). But even at this point the sinner is still in the grasp of sin. The burden of past sins is still bearing hard upon his heart. Further study reveals that God has designed "baptism" as that act which "washes away" sins and set us "into" Christ. By the action of baptism, we are "set apart" for God's service (Acts 22:16; Galatians 3:27; 1 Corinthians 1:2) Whenever a man stands before God, having fully obeyed through faith the commands of God's will, that person is *qualified*! What happens if one refuses to obey these simple commands of God? Obviously that person is not qualified, but is disqualified for service in God's kingdom.

Paul was thankful that God had "delivered" the believers. This refers to God's redeeming from the power and authority of darkness and sin. God has redeemed us; we have not redeemed ourselves! In fact, there is no possible way that we would ever be able to provide acceptable sacrifice for sin (Ephesians 2:8, 9).

Paul was thankful that God had "translated" the believers. This word refers to an ancient practice of the conquering nation transporting the inhabitants of the conquered territory into another state. In a similar manner, God has defeated Satan and conquered the power of the realm of darkness. Because of His victory, God takes those who formerly lived in Satan's territory and has now transplanted them into His state. The state into which believers are translated is the "kingdom." This kingdom is in existence at the present time and these believers in Colossae were translated into it; the Hebrews were receiving it (Hebrews 12:28); and John was "in it" (Revelation 1:9). The church and the kingdom are the same thing. Thus, whenever one is placed the body of Christ through obedient faith, that person becomes a member of Christ's church and a citizen of God's kingdom.

THOSE WHO ASSOCIATE WITH THE SUPREME SAVIOR DEMONSTRATE...
A DEEP APPRECIATION OF CHRIST'S SACRIFICE (1:13- 14)

Paul uses a title in reference to Christ which expresses the deep understanding and appreciation of God's sacrifice. Christ is referred to as the "Son of His love." Because of great love, God offered His beloved "Son" so that you and I could be qualified, delivered, and translated. There was no other way for these things to have been accomplished. What great pain must have struck God's heart as He realized that no other alternative existed for man's salvation. Yet, in His great goodness and mercy, God offered His only begotten Son! *"For while we were yet weak, in due season Christ died for the ungodly. For scarcely for a righteous man will one die: for peradventure for the good man someone would even dare to die. But God commendeth his own love toward us, in that, while we were yet sinners, Christ died for us"* (Romans 5:6-8). Can any other text in the Bible express better the deep love which God directed toward us than this one which details the offering of the "Son of His love?"

The appreciation of Paul for the sacrifice of Christ is seen as he emphasizes that "in whom we have our redemption, the forgiveness of our sins." It is only in Christ that salvation is found. Here again His supremacy is demonstrated. This sweetness of forgiveness cannot be found in any other name (Acts 4:12). The deep appreciation for Christ's sacrifice is stated by Peter in these words, "*Ye were redeemed, not with corruptible things, with silver or gold, from your vain manner of life handed down from yours father; but with precious blood, as of a lamb without blemish and without spot, even the blood of Christ*" (1 Peter 1:18, 19).

DRAWING IT ALL TOGETHER

There is a wonderful passage found in Daniel 1:8 which well serves to close our thoughts on this lesson. "Daniel made up his mind that he would not defile himself with the king's choice foods or with the wine which he drank . . . And Daniel continued . . ." Why was this Old Testament character so devoted? Because he shared a close association with his great God! This association enabled Daniel to overcome all obstacles and trials.

We have discovered a wonderful lesson in the midst of this prayer for the Colossians. Whenever Christ is our Supreme Savior, we will develop an association with Him that will influence all aspects of life. We will become deeply concerned and devoted about others. We will possess a desire that will be demonstrated very clearly. We will abound with thanksgiving for all that God has done for our souls. We will deeply appreciate the sacrifice of the Son of God's love!

Do you share this association today? What hinders you from receiving the great blessings which such an association offers?

REFLECTIONS & RESOLUTIONS

Reflections from our study of Colossians 1:9-14:

1. Reflect on the general principle of associations. What other passages of scripture stress the need to be careful in our associations? Why is this important?

2. Reflect on the four points discussed in this lesson. Which one is the most important to you? Why? Select one point which you feel to be the most important and find several other references that support it.

3. Reflect on the wonderful power source that is available to all who own Christ as the Supreme Savior. Why is it that we need a power source outside of ourselves to deal with matters in the following areas?

    a. To be "steadfast"
    b. To be "longsuffering"
    c. To be "joyful

4. Reflect on the three points in number three. How are they connected with each other? Is it possible to be steadfast and longsuffering but not joyful? How does joy have any connection with the other two?

Resolutions arising from our study of Colossians 1:9-14:

1. Resolve that you will develop an association with the Supreme Savior so that the four points in this lesson will be a part of your life.
2. Resolve to become more aware of the need to be devoted and concerned about others.

3. Resolve that you will learn to trust in God's power to assist you in becoming steadfast, longsuffering, and joyful.

= 5 =

THE SAVIOR'S SUPREMACY

"Who is the image of the invisible God, the firstborn of all creation; for in him were all things created, in the heavens and upon the earth, things visible and things invisible, whether thrones or dominions or principalities or powers; all things have been created through him, and unto him; and he is before all things, and in him all things consist. And he is the head of the body, the church: who is the beginning, the firstborn from the dead; that in all things he might have the preeminence. For it was the good pleasure of the Father that in him should all the fulness dwell; and through him to reconcile all things unto himself, having made peace through the blood of his cross; through him, I say, whether things upon the earth, or things in the heavens. And you, being in time past alienated and enemies in your mind in your evil works, yet now hath he reconciled in the body of his flesh through death, to present you holy and without blemish and unreprovable before him: if so be that ye continue in the faith, grounded and steadfast, and not moved away from the hope of the gospel which ye heard, which was preached in all creation under heaven; whereof I, Paul, was made a minister."
(Colossians 1:15-23)

I read the following account which provides an excellent illustration of our lesson text. In Leonardo DaVinci's famous painting of "The Last Supper," our Lord's hands are empty. It is in these empty hands that we find an impressive lesson. DaVinci dedicated three years to perfecting his masterpiece, determined that it would be his crowning work. Before the unveiling, he decided to show it to a friend and receive the friend's opinion. The friend looked at the painting and highly praised the skilled depiction. The friend remarked, "The cup in Christ's hand is especially beautiful. It will certainly draw the attention of each who gaze upon it!" At once DaVinci began to take a paintbrush and with quick, deft strokes soon had the cup completely erased from the canvas. The friend was amazed and asked, "Why? The cup was so beautiful. Why did you eliminate it?" The artist wanted all attention focused upon the Lord and would not tolerate anything to draw the viewer's attention away. Having removed the cup, he had to do something with the empty hand. The left hand was already outstretched just above the table, lifting as if to bless and command. Now the right hand was also empty, it was made to be outstretched in an inviting manner.

In the present section of Colossians, we are able to see how the pen of inspiration invites and commands its readers to look solely at the Supreme Savior. Paul's words clearly indicate that there should be no thing, no person, nor any created intelligence to take away the attention which Christ alone deserves!

The present text is an amazing passage. In fact, it is safe to state that the section we are now concerned with is THE MOST IMPORTANT PARAGRAPH OF SCRIPTURE found in Colossians, and perhaps in the entire Bible! This bold assertion can be easily supported. Within these nine verses the reader will find at least twenty-three references to Christ. When that number is compared with the total references to the Lord in the entire book, it will be found here is one-fourth of the references to Christ in this book. This surely is a most significant point to consider. Added to the many references to Christ in this paragraph, we are able to discover all that we must know in order to be eternally saved. Within these verses we are able to discover all of the essential doctrinal points that are associated with our Lord's life and duties. If the reader is still uncertain about the importance of this paragraph, perhaps at the conclusion it will be admitted.

The reason for Paul's penning this masterful description of Christ was due to the error confronting our brethren in Colossae. There were those who taught that the believers needed to believe in Christ, but they also needed to believe in other things. [See the lesson dealing with 2:16-23 for a description of these threats.] The believers were being told that the stars and planets were to be adored. They were being told that certain aspects of Judaism had to be followed. Thus, they were being told that Christ was important, *but* there were others things just as important. Paul confronts this error with an argument which stands unmatched. Paul's argument says-- "Jesus Christ is the only Person you need to follow. Do not look for any addition. Do not feel that with Him alone you are inadequate. Jesus Christ is the One and only One that believers need in order to be made complete!" If the Apostle could present the Savior's qualifications in such a way that Christ overshadowed all other contenders, surely the brethren would be convinced. This is exactly what Paul does in the present passage. We discover three points which establish beyond any question the supremacy of Christ Jesus.

JESUS CHRIST IS THE SUPREME SAVIOR
BECAUSE OF HIS DEITY (1:15, 19)

Here is a point which the Colossians needed to clearly understand. If Jesus Christ is divine [If He is God], then HE must be far superior to any other system or person. In order to establish the deity of Christ, Paul brings the following points to our attention.

First, Christ is the "IMAGE" of God! (v. 15a). He is the EIKON. The Greek word was used in reference to the images found on coins or portraits. It referred to a representation that had the exact likeness, or a precise reproduction. The word carried with it three ideas—resemblance, representation, and revelation. As Paul applies this word to Christ, a very significant fact is revealed. Christ IS NOT a mere copy. He is the representation, the likeness, the revelation of Almighty God! This likeness is referred to in Hebrews 1:3 by the phrase, "*the very image of his substance.*" So clear was this "image" that when Philip asked the Lord to show them God, Christ replied that they had a perfect revelation of God and needed nothing else. They had HIM! (cf. John 14:9). As this "image," Christ possessed the exact essence of Almighty God in heaven.

Second, Christ is the "FIRSTBORN" (v. 15b). This phrase has caused a great controversy among those who wish to deny the deity of Christ. Those who want to dethrone Christ misuse this phrase to teach that Christ was among "the first beings created by God." Such claim that Paul says Christ is the "firstborn"; therefore, He was created first. Such an erroneous concept is clearly exposed by looking at the way this term is used in the Bible. The term "firstborn" can be used in one of two ways as demonstrated by Exodus 4:22, 23. "*Then you shall say to Pharaoh, 'Thus says the Lord, Israel is My son, My firstborn.' So I said to you, 'Let My son go that he may serve Me'; but you have refused to let him go. Behold, I will kill your son, your firstborn.*" NASV

In this passage we are able to see the term "firstborn" referring to two different concepts: [1] It can refer to time sequence. Pharaoh's son was the "firstborn in the sense that he was first in time relation to the other children. [2] It can refer to position, honor, favor, and chosen uniqueness. This is the sense that Israel was God's "firstborn." As a nation she shared a chosen uniqueness with God. As Paul refers to Christ in verse 15b, he uses this second sense. Christ is God's "firstborn" in the sense of honor and chosen uniqueness. It is absurd to conclude that Christ was the first created being of God because Paul clearly states that Christ created ALL things. He did not create Himself! There is no other person who can be the firstborn of God but the Lord and Savior Jesus Christ!

Third, Christ contains the "FULNESS" of God (v. 19b). The verb "fulness" refers to something that is complete; nothing is lacking. By using this verb, Paul claims that Christ has all the qualities of God present in Him. Nothing is missing! God's nature, attributes, power, essence, and love are all in Christ. It is interesting to note that Paul says this fulness "dwells" in Christ. This is a most significant point to consider. The word "dwells" refers to a permanent home. God's "fulness" was a permanent quality in Christ; they were permanently at home in Him (cf. Philippians 2:6). No one else has ever had it said about them that the sum total of God's essence was a permanent quality with them—that is, no one but our Lord and Savior!

Fourth, Christ was "Preexistent" (vs. 17). Christ existed before anything! He testified to this fact as He said, *"Before Abraham was born, I am"* (John 8:58). That such a statement implied His preexistence and deity is seen in the attempt of the Jews to stone Him for making Himself equal with God.

Because of these four qualities, Paul could urge brethren at Colossae to follow the Supreme Savior only.

He is the Supreme Savior because of His deity. No angel, body of star, or human being could claim this fact and substantiate it. Only Christ could!

Two gentlemen were discussing the deity of Christ when one affirmed that if it were so, it should have been more explicitly stated in the Bible. The other asked, "How would you express it to make it unquestionable?" The other answered, "I would say that Jesus Christ is the true God." The other answered, "You are happy in the choice of your words, and they are the very words of inspiration! The Apostle John, speaking of Christ, says, *"This is the true God and eternal life"* (1 John 5:20).

JESUS CHRIST IS THE SUPREME SAVIOR BECAUSE OF
HIS AWESOME POWER (1:15-18, 20-22)

It is God's power that always demonstrates that He is the Supreme Sovereign of earth and the universe. Remember God's power demonstration in Egypt? Satan and man tried as best they could to reproduce the miraculous plagues but finally the magicians had to hang their heads and admit, *"This is the finger of God"* (Exodus 8:19). Eventually the Bible reads, *"The magicians could not stand before Moses"* (Exodus 9:11). God's power had triumphed over Satan's! Once again, the demonstration proved that God's power is so great that it is not a match for anyone.

In this paragraph, we once again find the fact that God's power is so awesome that it must be admitted. And in the text Paul is careful to show the Colossians that it is Christ who possesses this supreme might. Look at how the awesome power of Christ is described by Paul.

First, consider the POWER OF CREATION (v. 16). The Bible is clear in asserting that ONLY Christ Jesus possesses the power of creation (John 1:3, 10). Carefully consider how creation relates to Christ— "IN" Him creation finds it source; "THROUGH" Him creation was brought into being; "FOR" Him creation exists! One can never believe that Christ is the Supreme Savior and believe in evolution.

Second, consider the POWER OF COHESION (v. 17b). This is a most interesting point to consider. Christ possesses the power to hold "all things together." As Paul stood before the learned philosophers of Athens, he asserted that "*in Him we live and move and have our being*" (Acts 17:28). Christ's power to hold all things together is amazing. He is the one who keeps things from falling to pieces. There are those today who trust in astrology to keep their lives together. In fact, some people cannot make even a simple decision without consulting their "charts." But that behavior is ridiculous! It is foolishness in light of what Paul says here. The only One who can hold life together is Christ. The only ONE who can hold your family together is Christ. The old adage, "The family that prays together, stays together" only verifies what inspiration recorded centuries ago. The only ONE who holds our universe together is Christ. What will explain the order and pattern of unity of Nature? The only acceptable and reasonable answer is Christ Jesus. As one has ably stated, "He gives us a cosmos instead of a chaos!"

Third, consider His POWER TO CONQUER DEATH (v. 18b). Others have been raised from the dead only to die again; but Christ was the first to be raised with an incorruptible body. "*...Christ being raised from the death dieth no more; death no more hath dominion over him...*" (Romans 6:9). No one else is able to claim this.

Fourth, consider His POWER TO RECONCILE (vs. 20-22). Man has vainly tried and repeatedly failed to seek ways by which he can reconcile himself to Almighty God. We may try to do the best we can, but even then *"all our righteousness are as filthy rags"* (Isaiah 64:6, KJV). To find reconciliation with God we must look for means outside of ourselves. The only acceptable way is through Christ. Christ alone supplies the power which can reconcile man with God (cf. Ephesians 2:11-22). In the text, Paul points out that Christ's power to reconcile can accomplish: [1] *Peace*. He abolishes the cause of enmity and shows us the way to acceptance (vs. 20); [2] *Changed minds*. It is man's mind which must be changed if his will is to be pleasing unto God (v. 21); [3] *Perfect charact*er. Only by looking to Christ is it possible to become "holy and without blemish and unreprovable before him" (v. 22).

Notice that NO ONE but the Supreme Savior has the awesome power to accomplish these four things. Why should the Colossians trust in someone or something to do what Christ alone has the power to do? Pompey boasted that with one stamp of his foot he could rouse all Italy to arms. But Christ, by one word of His mouth, can summon the inhabitants of heaven, earth, and the undiscovered worlds, to His aid, or bring new creatures into existence to do His will!

JESUS CHRIST IS THE SUPREME SAVIOR BECAUSE OF
HIS POSITIONS (1:16, 18)

In a concise manner, the Apostle lists four positions which are held by Christ. As he lists these positions, it is emphasized that NO ONE but the Supreme Savior is able to rightfully possess these.

Christ is the Sovereign Ruler of the universe! As Paul surveys the various orders of the universe, he mentions each one. All who are in the material realm are subject to

Christ because He created them. Those who are in the spiritual realm are also subject to Christ because they too were created by Him. Notice how complete the list is—*"in the heavens and upon the earth, things visible and things invisible, whether thrones or dominions or principalities or powers; all things have been created through him, and unto him."* To those who were advocating following the heavenly starts, this point asks, "Why follow something that was created when you can follow the Someone who created them?" To those who were anxious to worship the angelic orders, this point asks, "Why worship that which was created to serve, when you could worship the One who created the angels to serve Him?" The universal Lordship of Christ is a position that no one can lay claim to except Christ Jesus. Why follow anyone else?

Christ is the Head of the church! (v. 18). His body is the church and as its head He provides and sustains life for the members of that body. As the head of the body, He makes the decisions. All decisions are according to the head's directions. As the head of the church, He give direction and guidance. And as the head of the church, He affords unity and enables the church to function with one purpose. There may be those today who claim to be the "head" of some church or denomination, but the Bible states plainly that Christ is the only head of HIS church. This position must be respected and submitted to in all practices.

Christ is the Beginning! (v. 18b). The word "beginning" refers to a "source." There have been those who have turned to Revelation 3:14 and read, Christ is *"the beginning of the creation of God."* They have wrongly concluded that Christ was created by God. But the word simply refers to a "source." Thus, Revelation 3:14 is simply stating that Christ is "the source of the creation of

God." Such understanding is in complete harmony with the inspired teaching of Paul in this paragraph. The word translated "beginning" can also refer to a "rule or authority" as in Luke 20:20. Therefore, our Lord occupies a position which shows us that He is the origin and source of life for the church and that He is the rule and authority for His church.

Christ is the firstborn from the dead! (v. 18c). The same title is found in Revelation 1:5. Once again Paul expresses the Savior's supremacy over the realm of death. By His glorious resurrection, HE is able to offer the source of life to His followers. No one else is able to hold this position.

DRAWING IT ALL TOGETHER

As Paul argues the supremacy of Christ, he bases his argument on a three-pronged attack. Christ is the Supreme Savior because of His deity. Christ is the Supreme Savior because of His awesome power. Christ is the Supreme Savior because of His glorious positions. In verse 23 we find a fitting exhortation. What will happen when we realize the supremacy of Christ? Paul says we will "*continue in the faith, grounded, and steadfast, and not moved away from the hope of the gospel.*" Acknowledging the preeminence of Christ (v. 18b), we can do little else than serve Him in earnest efforts.

Do you know the supremacy of Christ Jesus? Do you see the great significance of this paragraph of scripture? There is NO ONE ELSE who is qualified to be the Supreme Savior but Christ Jesus. Thus, let us follow the Lord's will. He is divine. He possesses awesome powers that will enable us to be perfected and stand acceptably before God. He alone is entitled to the glorious positions that are worthy of His great character.

Let us be careful that we do not become as the Colossian believers and try to place people and things on an equal plane with Jesus Christ. He is preeminent—no one else deserves to be on an equality with Him!

REFLECTIONS & RESOLUTIONS

Reflections from our study of Colossians 1:15-23:

1. Reflect on the three points discussed by Paul in our passage that verify the supremacy of Christ. Find other verses which unite in teaching...

    a. His deity
    b. His awesome power
    c. His glorious positions

2. Reflect on the Colossian failure to remember the preexistence of Jesus Christ. Why do you think they failed to remember? Are we in any danger of this today?

3. Reflect on the categories in verse 16. Why would some want to suggest that Christ was either equal with or inferior to these groups? Are there people today who want to do the same thing? How can this be done?

4. Reflect on verses 20-23. How is the pattern of reconciliation accomplished in Christ? How was "peace" with God made through the Savior's blood? Why must man's "mind" be changed before this reconciliation can take place?

5. Reflect on verse 23. Why will a realization of the Savior's supremacy change your life? Put into your own words what the following means....

a. "Continue in the faith"
b. "Grounded and steadfast"
c. "Not moved away from the hope of the gospel"

Resolutions arising from our study of Colossians 1:15-23:

1. Resolve that you will come to a greater understanding of the supremacy of Christ.

2. List three ways that you need to change to become more acceptable to the Supreme Savior. How will you go about making these changes?

3. Resolve that you will make sure that verse 23 helps you to live more acceptably to God.

= 6 =
ATTITUDES INSTILLED BY THE SUPREME SAVIOR

"Now I rejoice in my sufferings for your sake, and fill up on my part that which is lacking of the afflictions of Christ in my flesh for his body's sake, which is the church; whereof I was made a minister, according to the dispensation of God which was given me to you-ward, to fulfil the word of God, even the mystery which hath been hid for ages and generations: but now hath it been manifested to his saints, to whom God was pleased to make known what is the riches of the glory of this mystery among the Gentiles, which is Christ in you, the hope of glory: whom we proclaim, admonishing every man and teaching every man in all wisdom, that we may present every man perfect in Christ; whereunto I labor also, striving according to his working, which worketh in me mightily."
(Colossians 1:24-29)

During the War of 1812, the decisive battle was fought on Lake Erie. Commodore Perry announced the result to the government in these well-known words: "We have met the enemy and they are ours!" These words, spoken long ago, serve well to identify the attitude that is essential if Christians are to find victory over the wiles of Satan. However, many Christians fail to find victory in life because they have miserably failed to develop the attitudes which are essential to victory. In fact, because many believers have never developed the proper attitudes, they are forced to hang their heads and softly admit, "We have met the enemy, and WE ARE HIS!"

In our present text we find the Apostle Paul revealing some of the attitudes which are essential to victory in Christ. We are able to see just how crucial proper attitudes are in following the Supreme Savior. Paul's purpose for living was governed and directed by these attitudes. His life had meaning and his existence was important. Paul's life has happy, joy-filled, and heavenward bound because of these attitudes!

As the context is considered, we observe that Paul has just established the supremacy of Christ on three solid foundations: His deity, His power, and His positions. Now he set himself forth as one who recognizes the Savior's Supremacy and has responded to it. Because Christ is the Supreme Savior, Paul is a "minister" and a "steward." He performs these duties with delight because of the Savior's Supremacy!

If you are seeking victory over Satan; if you are searching for joy and delight that you know must be found in dedicated service to God's word; if you want to find meaning and purpose for life—look carefully at the passage before us. Only as you develop and maintain these attitudes of Paul will you find what you are looking for in life. We discover four important attitudes which are possessed by those who have Christ as their Supreme Savior. Carefully consider each one.

THE ATTITUDE TOWARD LIFE'S CIRCUMSTANCES:
REJOICING

This is a most interesting point to consider in the life of Paul. Upon several occasions he remarked that he found joy in the personal suffering for his brethren

(Philippians 1:12-14). The joy that he found is enhanced as Paul adds the word "In my sufferings." Paul refused to complain or to be depressed about the events of life. Here was a man who had every opportunity to let life beat him down and to rob him of joy; but he was stubborn enough to refuse to let it be done. Listen to what he says, "We live ... as sorrowful, yet always rejoicing, as poor, yet making many rich; as having nothing, and yet possessing all things (2 Corinthians 6: 9, 10; 2 Corinthians 4:7, 8). Paul could sit in a Roman prison and rejoice in sufferings because he knew his brethren would benefit. Notice carefully that in verse 24 Paul begins with a restricted view ("for your sake" – the brethren in Colossae), but then he broadens the scope to include the entire brotherhood ("for His body's sake, which is the church"). Paul was able to lift his eyes above the present, above the restricted, to see that his efforts and sufferings were of benefit to the entire church! Here he puts into practice that which he wrote, "*the members of the body, being many, are one body*" (2 Corinthians 12:12). His desire for the whole church was expressed later to Timothy, "*I endure all things for the elect's sake, that they also may obtain the salvation which is in Christ Jesus with eternal glory*" (2 Timothy 2:10). It was because of this marvelous attitude toward the situations of life that Paul possessed a great outlook. This outlook enabled him to be richly blessed. Whenever we compare the Apostle's attitude toward the ills of life with our attitudes, we find a great difference. Our brethren in the first century rejoiced "that they were counted worthy to suffer dishonor for the Name" (Acts 5:41). We are encouraged to develop this same attitude, "*suffer hardship with me, as a good soldier of Christ Jesus*" (2 Timothy 2:3).

Let us seriously look at this attitude of Paul and see how we need it in our lives. Let us look to the Savior's supremacy knowing that since He is supreme, he is able to use every circumstance in life to further His divine purpose. Since He is supreme, there is nothing that befalls us that cannot work toward the fulfillment of His purpose! *"And we know that to them that love God all things work together for good, even to them that are called according to his purpose* (Romans 8:28). We, as Paul, are not assured that everything that happens to us will be "good;" but we are assured that no matter what happens, God is going to use it to further His purpose. This established truth ought to cause us to "rejoice" even when everything is "going against us." What a beautiful attitude! And it results from knowing that Christ Jesus is the Supreme Savior.

THE ATTITUDE TOWARD DUTIES:
"I DO MY SHARE!" (NASB)

Here is a point I really like—Paul did *his* part; he did not leave it for anyone else to do! This expression refers to certain duties which Paul understood were his. These duties had been assigned to him because he had become a child of God. As the text is examined, it is found that Paul recognized his duties were in four areas.

First, he had duties toward the church (vs. 24, 25). He was made a "minister" or servant to the church. His labors were designed to be spent in their "sake." He sought to "fill up" that which was lacking in the church.

Second, he had duties toward his brethren (vs. 25, 28, 29). As the verses are considered, we see Paul knew he had the responsibility to preach, teach, counsel, and guide his fellow brethren with tender love and concern. He said that his primary duty toward believers was that of presenting *"every man perfect in Christ."*

Third, he had duties toward the world (vs. 25-28). As a Christian, Paul realized that his primary duty to those in the world was to make the wonderful gospel message known. As the New American Standard Version reads, *"That I might fully carry out the preaching of the word of God"* (v. 25b). As he taught the gospel, he was very careful to show his listeners that the only hope of salvation is found in Christ Jesus. Paul also realized that his duties to the world were universal in scope. He could not afford to limit or restrict his preaching to one section of the world or to one race of people. In verse 28 the three-fold repetition of *"every man"* is most significant. EVERY man has a right to hear the gospel preached. Earlier in verse 23 and also in verse 6 Paul referred to his universal obligation of preaching the gospel of Christ.

Fourth, he had duties toward God (vs. 25, 29). He was a "steward" of God. The word "dispensation" comes from a compound Greek word referring to a "house-ruler." This was the servant who was given the responsibility to see that all things in the household were conducted in the proper manner. As Paul uses this expression, he reveals to the readers that he is aware that he shared a very important position (cf. 1 Corinthians 4:1-5). As a steward of God, he must be faithful; he must exert energy. He knew that "woe" was awaiting him if he did not respond properly (1 Corinthians 9:16, 17).

Paul could look at each of these areas of service (duties toward the church, his brethren, the world, and God) and affirm in a very confident way, "I am doing my share!" This is a good point to consider. We should ask ourselves, "Am I doing MY share?" Do you wait for someone else to act on a pressing need or do you accept the fact that you share a part in the duty and willingly do your share? There are many who use this phrase as a "cop-out." For example, a need arises in a local congregation and this need is announced. There are several members who are more than qualified to meet that need; but each respond, "I will not do that because I am already doing MY share." How do you think Paul would have reacted? His expression is no excuse for evading further duties. In fact, he leaves his responsibility in each of the four areas open. His "share" is always increasing! Again, ask yourself, "Am I doing my fair share of the work load?"

Discussion of these four duties is a very important lesson, but we are able to discover an equally important lesson in seeing how Paul performed these duties. From this text we are able to see that these duties performed without the appropriate attitude are worthless. Paul's words detail for us HOW these duties are performed. Look closely at the attitudes which you and I must demonstrate as we do our share of the Lord's work.

Paul responded WILLINGLY. As we read the expression, "I do my share," we are impressed with his willingness. No one had to prod, or beg, or urger him. He did it willingly! Whenever a need is expressed in your local congregation, do you respond in this willing manner?

Paul responded UNSELFISHLY. His primary objective was the betterment of his brethren. In verse 24, the word "for" literally means "in the interest of." In the "interest of" his brethren, Paul was willing to accept these duties. What about you? When a need is expressed, do you serve to be seen of men and receive the approval of men? How content and satisfied would you be with performing a task knowing that no one would ever know? Paul was unselfish; he did not really care who knew as long as his brethren were helped!

Paul responded EARNESTLY. In verse 29 the words "labor" and "strive" refer to the Apostle's efforts. These are two interesting words. They are often associated with the athletic contests which required steady toil and intense concentration of the body. The contestants would often be exhausted and weary because of their labor and straining. As Paul applies these words to himself, we see a most interesting point revealed. His duties often required him to labor to the point of weariness and exhaustion; but he kept on! It is also interesting to note that he is using the present tense in verse 29. Thus, he indicates that even then, in the Roman jail, he was striving for his brethren (cf. 2:1). In later writings Paul would use these terms to express his determined efforts to receive the rewards of Heaven (1 Timothy 4:10). Paul would agree with the old evangelist who remarked, "I am weary in work, but never weary of it!"

How do you perform your duties in the Lord's kingdom? Our age is one of "quick fixes." If you lack energy and vigor, you can take a vitamin product and in a matter of minutes (so it is suggested) you are ready to wind up the day with enough energy to take on anything. But in this text, we discover that the only way we can find energy in the Lord's work is to develop this attitude of earnest labor. We must become so devoted to the Supreme Savior that we will see the urgency to "labor" and "strive" for our fellow brethren and those who are presently lost outside of Christ. If you want to find joy in life, then labor and strive for others! Devote time and energy to help others overcome the world and to assist them in finding the blessed assurance that is "in Christ."

Paul responded RESPONSIBLY. Divine duties must be accepted and performed in a responsible way. God will never tolerate the irresponsible servant. From the passage, we are able to discover three points that are essential to this responsible performance. To be a responsible servant you must speak with wisdom. Paul made sure that his speech and teaching was with "*all wisdom.*" This wisdom is described for us in James 3:13-18. It leads ones to live a good life. It causes one to speak so that the following traits are present: purity, peaceable, gentle, easily reasoned with, merciful, consistent, and without wavering in convictions. The child of God who seeks to perform his duties acceptably will know that wisdom governs actions. Associated with this wisdom Paul says is speaking "ALL" of the truth. Paul was careful to preach "all of the truth," not just a portion. He wanted to make men "complete" and he knew that a partial gospel would never do this. It is unfortunate that there are some who honestly think that they do not have to teach all of God's wisdom to perfect men in Christ.

Finally, the responsible servant recognizes his personal obligation to God. Carefully examine verses 24 and 25 and see how Paul was impressed with his personal obligation. Paul knew that it was a matter of "I" not "you," "he," and "she." To Paul it was "I rejoice," "I fill up," "I was made." There is not a single believer alive today that does not share the need to perform in the same personal way. We are faced with the urgency of accepting personal responsibility for obeying the divine duties. Will we respond as responsibly as Paul? Do you sense the urgency of the emphatic "I" as Paul did?

Paul responded and performed COMPLETELY. As you read this paragraph, pay close attention to the many references where Paul made sure he was obeying these duties in a complete way. He wanted to be sure that nothing was lacking. He said, "I do my share," "I . . . fully carry out the preaching." He was concerned about "every man." His objective was "completion" or "perfection." He was not going to be satisfied with anything short of doing the tasks completely! Thus, we have noticed the duties which Paul realized were his to perform, and the attitudes which dictated how he responded to obeying these commands.

During the dark day of 1780, in Connecticut the candles were lighted in many house, and domestic fowls went to their roost. The people thought the day of Judgment had come. The legislature was then in session at Hartford. The House of Representatives adjourned. In the Council it was also proposed. Colonel Davenport objected to the adjournment saying, "The day of Judgment is either approaching, or it is not. If it is not, there is no cause for adjourning; if it is, I choose to be found doing my duty. I wish, therefore, that candles be brought in and business continued." Let us have the same resolve about performing our duties. Only as we view the supremacy of Christ in the exact manner that Paul did will we be able to possess these attitudes of Paul.

THE ATTITUDE TOWARD OTHERS:
LOVE AND CONCERN

Throughout this section, and the next (2:1-5), we are able to see the wonderful attitude of Paul toward his brethren. Briefly consider how Paul demonstrated love and concern to others. He was willing to use himself for the benefit of others (v. 25). He desired to reveal the divine mystery of God's plan of salvation to all men so that they would be able to mature in the faith (v. 28). He exerted energy and actually "wore himself out" in doing those things which would assist others in saving their souls (v. 29).

Whenever we possess this attitude toward others, we will be able to offer the support and encouragement which aids in developing and perfecting faith. Those who demonstrate this attitude are the ones who recognize the supremacy of Christ and are anxious to emulate His divine love, concern, and acceptance.

THE ATTITUDE TOWARD GOD'S WILL:
COMPLETE TRUST

Paul's confidence in the will of God was unshakeable! This is perhaps one of the greatest points in Paul's life. No matter what happened to him, he knew that God's will would be furthered. We have already examined this faith in discussion of 1:1, 2. To the Apostle there was no questioning the divine care and providence. *"For it is God who worketh in you both to will and to work, for his good pleasure"* (Philippians 2:13). In the present text, Paul once again expresses an attitude of complete trust in the will of God. He knows that God's will is final. It was God's will which led to the revelation of how man can be saved (v.27). He knew that God's will held incomparable riches (v. 27). In 2 Corinthians 12: 9, 10, Paul reveals that a trust in the will of God will provide tremendous strength, enabling us to overcome the "thorns" of life. Certainly, we should see how an attitude will result from an outgrowth of knowing Christ as the Supreme Savior. If Christ is the Supreme Savior, as He most certainly is (1:15-23), He is worthy of rewarding any trust placed in Him.

Let us place a similar trust and confidence in the will of God. If we can do this, we will never be put to shame (Romans 5:3-5a).

DRAWING IT ALL TOGETHER

Didn't Paul possess four wonderful attitudes? As he faced the circumstances of life, there was JOY regardless of what happened. As he faced duties he could say, "I do my share!" And he did it with such wonderful attitudes that many of us are put to shame. As he looked at others, he guided his words and actions with love and concern. And, as he looked toward the will of God, he shared a confident trust!

How can we have these attitudes? Verse 27 gives us the answer. We must have "Christ in us" because only He is the hope of glory! But before we can have "Christ in us", we must be found "in Him." We are found in Him only as we obey His revealed will. This means that in obedient faith we are saved by confessing, repenting, and being immersed for the forgiveness of past sins (Luke 13:3; Matthew 10:32; Acts 22:16; Galatians 3:27).

Consider your attitude today. Can you send the victorious message, "We have met the enemy and he is ours!" or must you be forced to concede the struggle by admitting, "I have met the enemy and I am his!" If you want to find purpose and power for life, begin to develop these four points in your life. Look to Christ Jesus as the Supreme Savior!

REFLECTION & RESOLUTIONS

Reflections from our study of Colossians 1:24-29:

1. Reflect over the four attitudes discussed in this lesson and write down why they would give you victory in life.

2. List each of the four attitudes revealed in the text. Which one do you think is the most important? Why? How can this one, that you selected, give meaning and purpose to life?

3. Reflect on the four broad points that Paul was responsible for performing. Is it possible for one to ever say, "I have done everything I can in this area?" Discuss the excuse that is commonly used by those who say, "I am doing MY share and will not do any more." Of the four duties listed, is there any one which is more important than the others?

4. Reflect on how Paul performed the four duties to the church, his brethren, the world, and to God. Which of these is the most important to you? Which of these is the least important? Think of an illustration for each of the ways that characterized Paul's service— willingly, unselfishly, earnestly, responsibly, and completely.

5. Reflect on Paul's attitude of complete trust in God's will. Why do you think this concept is so often expressed by Paul? How does this attitude result in a happy, joy-filled life?

Resolutions arising from our study of Colossians 1:24-29.

1. Resolve that you will begin developing each of these four attitudes in your life.

2. Resolve that you will immediately begin serving God in the exact manner that the Apostle Paul did.

3. Resolve that you will find a supreme victory because you possess the Supreme Savior.

4. Resolve that your singular purpose in life will be that of the apostles—to "present every man perfect in Christ."

— 7 —
REDESIGNED BY THE SUPREME SAVIOR

"For I would have you know how greatly I strive for you, and for them at Laodicea, and for as many as have not seen my face in the flesh; that their hearts may be comforted, they being knit together in love, and unto all riches of the full assurance of understanding, that they may know the mystery of God, even Christ, in whom are all the treasures of wisdom and knowledge hidden. This I say that no one may delude you with persuasiveness of speech. For though I am absent in the flesh, yet I am with you in the spirit, joying and beholding your order, and the steadfastness of your faith in Christ."
(Colossians 2:1-5)

As John the Immerser preached his message of the Messiah's nearness, he challenged those who came to be immersed, *"Bring forth fruits worthy of repentance!"* (Matthew 3:8). As our blessed Lord taught, He observed the truth, *"By their fruits ye shall know them"* (Matthew 7:16a). The point of both these proclamations is that change was necessary. It was rightly expected from those who sought the salvation of the Messiah.

There once was a servant who had to be constantly reprimanded by her employer because she did not follow instructions to sweep under the doormat. This servant was converted by hearing and obeying the simple gospel message. Her employer noticed immediately a change in her attitudes and general conduct. Hearing remarks about this change, the servant seemed pleased—but also puzzled, wondering what action had caused the change to be noticed. She asked her employer and received the answer, "Why, you have been sweeping under the doormat!" It is often the little things which call people's attention to the fact that the supremacy of the Lord Christ has changed our attitudes and lives. The little things add up to make a drastic difference.

As Paul writes this section of the Colossian epistle, he calls attention to the fact that the Savior has drastically redesigned his life. In the last section (1:24-29) we were able to see the intense affection and desire for the Lord's church in general terms. Now Paul turns to focus in specific terms as to his labors for the brethren in Colossae. The careful reader is able to see the Apostle's heart opened for close inspection and his inner attitudes revealed.

As you read these verses, you have to be impressed with the change that is evident in Paul's life. Do you remember the "old" Paul described in Acts 8:1-3? This was the man who was "*a blasphemer, and a persecutor, and injurious*" (1 Timothy 1:13). He had no affection or desire for the church at all. But now, contract the Paul of Acts 8 with the Paul of Colossians 2:1-5 and you will find a changed man. What can account for this change? What prompted the reform? What was it that redirected his attitudes, life, and goals? One word is sufficient to answer all of these questions—CHRIST! Paul came to realize the supremacy of the Lord Jesus Christ. Listen, "*And the grace of our Lord abounded exceedingly with faith and love which is in Christ Jesus. "I have been crucified with Christ; and it is no longer I that live, but Christ liveth in me: and that life which I now live in the flesh I live in faith, the faith which is in the Son of God, who loved me, and gave himself up for me*" (Galatians 2:20). In the life of Paul, we find the best illustration of the Savior's power to redesign man's will.

From a close study of the lesson text, we are able to see specific ways that the Supreme Savior will redesign the lives of those who "trust and obey" His divine will.

UNDERSTANDING CHRIST'S SUPREMACY WILL CHANGE THE WAY...
YOU FEEL ABOUT BELIEVERS (VS. 1, 4, 5A)

You will "strive for" them (v. 1). The Greek word that is translated "strive" is most interesting. It means to "struggle, contend, or fight." It is found in 1:29. One of the versions renders it as "strenuously exerting." While even in a Roman prison, Paul was agonizing over his brethren in Colossae and in Laodicea. This was done through his prayers. Paul's prayers were not quick, flippant thoughts. As the Apostle prayed, he literally fought and struggled for those in his prayers. Here is a reference to a deep and prolonged intercession for another. This is a most beautiful trait in Paul's life. Paul consumed time and energy and emotion in earnest prayers for believers he had never met.

This trait is greatly needed in the Lord's church today. We need brethren who will spend emotion and energy in strenuous prayers for the welfare of fellow believers! Look carefully at your own prayer habits and answer these questions. Whom have you "fought for" in prayers this week? How often do you "struggle" for a brother in prayers? When was the last time that you got down on your knees and spent time in deep intercession for a fellow believer?

A new believer in Christ was on the verge of going back into the world's habits. One of his fellow members realized the impending danger and tried several times to visit with him but never found him at home. The new convert missed several assemblies and the concerned brother could not find him at home. Finally, contact was made and the concerned member said, "Joe, I have tried several times to contact you, but we could never seem to connect. I want you to know that I have really been fighting for you in my prayers because I do not want you to go back to the life you have left!" Through the encouragement and fellowship expressed in this way, the new convert was strengthened in his resolve to remain steadfast to the Savior. If Christ is your Supreme Savior, you will see the urgency of developing and maintaining this kind of prayer habit that Paul had.

You will be concerned about the spiritual steadfastness of brethren (v. 4). Paul mentions two points which show us his grave concern for the brethren in Colossae. *First,* the word "delude" suggests the idea of being deceived by a plausible argument that appears to be based upon fact; but in truth it is founded upon falsehood. This word is sometimes used by the ancients to describe a lawyer who is defending a criminal who is guilty. But, by disguising his arguments to appear as truth, the jury is deceived and the guilty part is allowed to go free. *Second,* the phrase "persuasiveness of speech" reveals Paul's concern for the Colossians. This speech is the kind that is enticing, attractive, and appealing. However, it is not based upon facts.

When these two points are considered, we are able to see that Paul was concerned that some "fast talking, smooth-tongued" teacher would blind his brethren to the truth of Christ. An equal concern is demanded in our modern day. We are constantly around those who wish to add a new doctrine to the Lord's commands. We have seen innocent people accept denominationalism as "God-ordained." We are bombarded by those who claim that the answers to all of life's trials are found in astrology or the occult. Those who hold Christ as the Supreme Savior will share Paul's concern about the welfare of fellow brethren. Look at these passages and see how this concern is expressed—Ephesians 4:14; Romans 16:18; 1 Corinthians 2:4, 5.

You will realize the beautiful bond of universal fellowship (v. 5a). Paul shared a relationship with believers that distance could never sever! This is a great contrast to some brethren who meet in the same building but are so distant from one another that they never know the joy of fellowship in Christ's church. Our Savior is the universal Sovereign, and as His body we are members of one another. This body is not limited to just your home congregation, or the congregations of the Lord's church in your city or town. No matter how far we may be separated from one another, there is a beautiful bond which binds each of us with one another. It is because of this blessed bond that, even while in distant travel, fellow members of the Lord's body can come together and enjoy a period of worship and praise that is unmatched.

To illustrate how the bond of fellowship is universal, the following is told. A Hindu and a New Zealander met upon the deck of a ship where they had been converted to Christ. They had turned from their heathenism, and were brothers in Christ; but they could not speak to each other. They pointed to their Bible, shook hands, smiled, but that was all. At last, a happy thought occurred to the Hindu. With sudden joy he exclaimed, "Hallelujah!" The New Zealander, in delight, cried out, "Amen!" These two words, not found in their own native tongues, were to them the beginning of "one language and one speech." Truly this is the essence of the brotherhood shared by all members of the body of Christ—all barriers are removed and all former prejudices are slowed worked away so that all brethren stand united and joyfully speak the same thing! As we think of our brethren in distant lands, we, as Paul, although *"being absent in body but present in spirit"* (1 Corinthians 5:3a) will strive in prayers for their well-being.

UNDERSTANDING CHRIST'S SUPREMACY WILL CHANGE THE WAY...
YOU VIEW THE CHURCH (VS. 2, 3)

First, you will see the church becoming a source of strength (v. 2a). The word "comforted" comes from a Greek verb which has a double meaning of comfort and to exhort or urge. Thus, Paul says the church becomes the source to hearten, to encourage, to strengthen the members of Christ's body! Perhaps the word "fortified" describes the concept expressed here better to us. If we fail to grasp the meaning of this concept, we will fall prey to the wiles of Satan. Failure to be fortified by the church will result in our becoming sad and unnerved in life. But, if we have this concept expressed by Paul, we will find a most comforting view of the Lord's church. We will see the periods of assembly not only as opportunities to praise and glorify God in a united effort, but we will see them as a wonderful period of time to assemble and exhort and provoke one another to remain steadfast against Satan's devices! We will be fortified against the fiery darts of distress, discouragement, sadness, and temptation. It is interesting to observe that this same word is used to describe Barnabas in Acts 4:36. As you look at Acts 11: 22, 23 you are able to see how he "comforted" the disciples in Antioch. He challenged, comforted, fortified, and strengthened. Those who own Christ as the Supreme Savior will be changed in the way they view the church. Has your view of the church changed?

Second, you will see the church becoming a close-knit family unit (v. 2b). This "knitting is a beautiful expression of the bond found in the Lord's church (cf. Ephesians 4:16; Colossians 2:19). Members of the church who know the supremacy of the Savior will literally become "welded together."

There are some implications which arise from this thought. Welding causes a dependence upon one another. It causes a close harmony with other members; for what can be welded together unless compatibility exists. There will be one definite purpose which all parts are concerned with developing. There will be a bonding which, if not present, will make the effort useless. And, from a multiple number in the beginning, there will result one cohesive piece in the end. This "knitting" is a beautiful way to express the wonderful unity found in Ephesians 4. Just as in the knitting of any piece of material, there is an interlocking of threads. Paul tells us that in the church this interlocking is permanently insured by "love" being present.

Third, you will see the Lord's church become the sole source of assurance (vs. 2b, 3). Paul looks at the church and sees that it along is the way for believers to find assurance in life. Often believers are insecure and uncertain about their relationship with God because they have failed to see the church with a view from the Supreme Savior. So important is the church to the plan of God that as Paul views it, he finds in it everything that gives meaning to your life. However, this meaning is realized only as Christ is received as the Supreme Savior. Carefully study Ephesians 1:3-23 and you will read a most amazing discussion on the magnificence of the Lord's church. By looking in the present text, we are able to see two things which are in the church and provide assurance for believers. The church possesses the knowledge that leads to understanding (v. 2b) And, the church possesses the means by which we can have access to ALL treasures (v. 3).

Fourth, you will begin to view the church as "universal" instead of local (v. 1b). Paul's Supreme Savior was over all the world and the Lord's church was located over all the world. In each location there were those who worshipped faithfully according the Lord's instructions.

Because of his universal understanding of the church, Paul confessed, *"there is that which presseth upon me daily, anxiety for all the churches"* (2 Corinthians 11:28). We can never realize the universal brotherhood of believers until we realize the universal supremacy of Christ Jesus.

UNDERSTANDING CHRIST'S SUPREMACY WILL CHANGE…
YOUR STANDARD OF JOY (VS. 5)

Paul's joy stemmed from one thing—seeing his brethren faithfully following Christ's supremacy. Two military metaphors are used by Paul to show his joy at how the Colossians were remaining faithful. They were in "order." This word refers to the unity of a military unit. It has been rendered as "orderly array." They were demonstrating a "steadfastness." This word refers to a solid line that marches into battle to penetrate and defeat the opposing warriors. The word has been rendered as a "solid front." Paul joyed because the brethren in Colossae were a group of compact soldiers who were standing firm in their position. They had strength and power from the solidity of the line they present to error.

It should be of great concern to us if our joy is stirred by things other than this one. What causes you the greatest joy in life? What is the one thing that makes you the happiest? Can you say, with Paul, that you are the happiest when you hear about a local congregation that is standing firm in the faith? Our standard of joy will tell us how we view the Supreme Savior. Once we come to know Christ as the Supreme Savior, we will find joy in the faithful devotion of others!

DRAWING IT ALL TOGETHER

After these thoughts, ask yourself— "Do I sweep under the door mat now?" How has your life changed? In these brief verses, we have been able to see three great changes that must be evident in the life of a person who realizes that Jesus Christ is the Supreme Savior. These three changes will affect a redesigning of attitudes and actions in life. There will be changes because your association and feelings about believers will be redesigned. There will be changes because your standard of joy has been redesigned.

Paul's struggles for these brethren are revealed so that they would realize the seriousness of their situation. Why was Paul's life redesigned? Why is there such a great contrast between the Paul of Acts 8 and the Paul of Colossians 2? *Because he had found and obeyed the Supreme Savior!*

REFLECTIONS & RESOLUTIONS

Reflections from our study of Colossians 2:1-5:

1. Look carefully over the fact that Savior will redesign your life once you obey His will. How is this most often demonstrated in life? In what specific ways have you been "redesigned" by Christ?

2. Reflect on the three ways suggested that we are changed in regard to fellow believers. Which of the three is the most impressive to you? Do you think believers "strive" enough for others in prayers? Why? How can we show fellow believers our concern about their steadfastness? Think of an illustration which shows how the beautiful bond of fellowship is found in the church?

3. Reflect on how Christ's supremacy changes the way we think about the church. How can the church "fortify" you? How can we become a closer "knit" family? Think about the importance of the church and the assurance it affords. Do you think we stress these two points enough? Find other passages which stress the church's importance. Why do you think there are some who think the church is not important?

4. Reflect on your standard of joy. Why should we find joy in the faithfulness of believers? What "things" often cause us to replace the standard of joy suggested by Paul in verse 5b? How can we deal with these "things" effectively?

Resolutions arising from our study of Colossians 2:1-5:

1. Resolve that you will strengthen your affection toward believers in Christ. Set three specific things you will do.

2. Resolve that you will study in greater detail to appreciate the importance of the Lord's church.

3. Resolve that you will not allow anything to usurp the standard of joy found in verses 5b.

═ 8 ═
LIVING LIFE WITH THE SUPREME SAVIOR

"As therefore ye received Christ Jesus the Lord, so walk in him, rooted and builded up in him, and established in your faith, even as ye were taught, abounding in thanksgiving. Take heed lest there shall be any one that maketh spoil of you through his philosophy and vain deceit, after the tradition of men, after the rudiments of the world, and not after Christ: for in him dwelleth all the fulness of the Godhead bodily, and in him ye were also circumcised with a circumcision not made with hands, in the putting off of the body of the flesh, in the circumcision of Christ; having been buried with him in baptism, wherein ye were also raised with him through faith in the working of God, who raised him from the dead. And you being dead through your trespasses and the uncircumcision of your flesh, you, I say, did he make alive together with him, having forgiven us all our trespasses; having blotted out the bond written in ordinances that was against us, which was contrary to us: and he hath taken it out of the way, nailing it to the cross; having despoiled the principalities and the power, he made a show of them openly, triumphing over them in it."
(Colossians 2:6-15)

It is reported that during the Civil War a certain Captain Burke was mortally wounded. Being taken to the field hospital he was asked, "How does it seem to you to be struck down with all of your hopes and prospects cut far short? Is it hard for you to give up life and leave your young family at your age?" He replied, "It has come suddenly, but I feel prepared. I have lived close to my

Savior in the Army and have tried to square all accounts with him each night." His wife was able to go and nurse him. Sometimes his mind would wander, but his wife would calm him by saying, "My dear, Jesus is here and that is all you need." His assured reply was, "You are right, that is all I want...All I want..." Such a life well illustrates the great blessings that are found in the person who lives in a close relationship with the Supreme Savior.

In the present passage we are able to discover how wonderful it is to live life with the Supreme Savior. Paul shows his readers that if they practice devotion to Christ there will be a great reward. The Apostle encourages his readers to make sure that they are living with the Savior so that this reward will be given to them. There are four points which are offered by Paul in this passage. These four points must be understood and practiced if we are to live life with the Savior. In observing the context, the following points are noted. Paul has opened his heart to the Colossian believers and has shown them his tender care and devotion (1:3-14; 1:24-25). Having demonstrated that he truly cared for them, Paul now turns to address the error which faces his brethren.

From a casual reading of chapter two, the following characteristics of the error are found. It was a philosophy of men that was patterned after the traditions of me (2:8). It contained various aspects of Judaism (2:11-18). It probably encouraged the worship of angels (2:18). And it enforced strict rules of self-denial (2:20). Each of these alone would pose a grave threat. But when taken together, they present a tremendous challenge to the believer's faith. Paul's task was to show his brethren that they did not need to submit to these facts. Submission must be given to Christ only! Paul must demonstrate that those who live their lives with the Savior will be far better than those who attempt to add or subtract from His supremacy. Look closely now and see how the life that is lived with the Supreme Savior is far better than anything else available.

THE BEGINNING

In 2:6, 12 we are able to see how this life lived with the Savior begins. It begins by our "receiving" Christ Jesus. It is very unfortunate that this word "receive" has become abused and distorted in our modern day. The word is biblical and can be found often in the New Testament (cf. 1 Corinthians 15:1; John 1:12). The word refers to the transmitting or safeguarding of tradition. Paul uses it in the sense that the apostolic teachings of Jesus Christ had been received and were in safe keeping with the Colossians. The Colossians had "received" the gospel message of Christ as they listened and obeyed the preaching of Epaphras (Colossians 1:7). It should be pointed out, in light of the sad perversion of the modern usage, that this manner of "receiving" Christ means more than simply hearing the gospel preached. The message must be heard; but the word denotes action in response to the message. *Something must be done!* There must be an effect that continues after the message had been heard.

By a close examination, we are able to discover HOW the Colossian brethren "received" Christ as Lord. *First*, as already mentioned, they heard the gospel preached by faithful Epaphras; and upon hearing it, they believed (1:4-7). But this hearing and believing was not all they did. They changed their lives so that a drastic difference was evident.

This drastic change evidences the *second* step in receiving Christ. It shows they repented (1:10). This is found in 2:11 where Paul uses the term "circumcision." Under the old dispensation, the covenant mark was circumcision of every male member. This was a physical, outward sign that the male belonged to the Abrahamic covenant. But under the New Testament the old manner of marking followers was changed. There was to be a new circumcision not made with hands. This was to affect the heart of all members. Having their heart circumcised, their entire lives were to demonstrate that they had severed the past and now lived entirely new lives. This decision to remove one's self from the past is found in repentance—which naturally comes when the gospel is heard and believed. But just hearing, believing, and repenting was not all the brethren in Colossae did in "receiving" Christ as Lord.

One further action was required. They had to be buried because they had died; and they needed to be raised because of the new relationship they were in with God. The burial and resurrection are beautifully stated in 2:12 where Paul refers to baptism. It was impossible for the Colossians to "walk in the new life" having "received Christ" until they had been buried. If such was true, then it certainly remains true for our time.

How can we walk in the "new" life until we have "died" and have been "buried" with Christ? It is significant to notice that Paul does not spend much discussion on the necessity of baptism in this passage simply because it was generally accepted. Should one be honest enough to sit down with Colossians 2:6-12 and read the verses without thought to any preconceived notion regarding how one is to be "raised" with Christ, the plain pattern of New Testament salvation would be unmistakable.

We must be careful to look seriously at this point. If we want to live life with the Supreme Savior, we must begin exactly as those in the ancient city of Colossae did. We must "receive Christ as Lord!"

THE DEVOTION

As verses 6 and 7 are studied, it will be discovered that there is one encompassing action which results when we "receive Christ Jesus the Lord." This action is described as a "walk" (v. 6b). The Apostle says in essence, "Since you have heard the wonderful gospel Word and believed its message which caused you to repent and be immersed, it is only natural that you will walk in Him." The word "walk" is a favorite expression of Paul's. He uses it often as a metaphor of the daily life of the believer. It suggests a steady progress—a patient going onward, to the final destination. In verse 6 it is used in the present tense and suggests a continuous action. The walk is never to cease! Every person "walks" through life. Some follow God while others follow Satan. Those who are careful to "receive" Christ will also be careful to walk "in him." That simply means—in every part of life we will not go anywhere, say anything, or do anything that is not proper because our Lord is walking right by our side.

The following story illustrates well how our "walk" affects the way we live:

"Father" said Clara, "I never could understand how the same wind can take ships in such different directions. There goes one in toward port, and there goes another out to sea."

The father smiled and then replied, "It all depends upon the position of the sails, dear."

Such is true with our walk in life. It all depends on the set of our sails. Some sail heavenward while others sail toward destruction. The breeze that carries one to heaven's rewards is strong, determined devotion while that which carries others toward destruction is the rejection and refusal of devotion. Let us be extremely careful to have our sails set to receive and be carried by that breeze of steadfast devotion which is spoken of by Paul as a "walk in Him."

The godly walk is further discussed in verse 7. The Colossians needed to develop this walk and Paul now tells them how it is to be developed. *First*, there was a "rooting" in Him. This "rooting" refers to an action that happened in our past and was a once-for-all event. This rooting took place whenever we were placed in Christ; thus, it occurred at the time we "received" Christ in verse 6 (cf. Galatians 3:27; Romans 6:3). Thus, they had been rooted in Him and should never become unrooted. In Ephesians 3:17 we find the soil in which we are to be rooted. It is "love." Without this proper soil we will never be able to live a life with the Supreme Savior. It is by love that we have the opportunity to be saved (John 3:16). And it is by love that we obey the will of God in order to find salvation (John 14:15). If we are not rooted in love, or if we have been improperly rooted, we will never be able to live with the Supreme Savior.

Second, there must be a "building up!" This word is found in the present tense and conveys the idea of growing and developing on a day-by-day basis. We were once-for-all rooted; but we are built up day-by-day. It is a reference to spiritual progress in the Christian life. As the Hebrew author said, "*Wherefore leaving the doctrine of the first principle of Christ, let us press on unto perfection...*" (Hebrews 6:1). If we want to live a life with the Supreme Savior, we must make sure that there is steady growth, progress, and development.

Third, there must be "establishing by faith!" Paul refers to the inner solidity, stability, or firmness. Those who seek to live with the Supreme Savior will become firm in what they believe, in what they stand for, and in the usual behavior of daily living. This point stresses the need for ALL to become stronger in the faith. Brother David Lipscomb has made the following comment on this phrase and his clear comment describes this point:

> *A progressive increase of faith is the condition of all Christian progress. The faith which is already the firmest is still capable of and needs strengthening. Its range can be enlarged, its tenacity increased, and its power over heart and life reinforced. The eye of faith is never so keen but that it may become more long-sighted; its grasp never so close that it may not be tightened; its realization never so solid but that it may become more substantial; this continued strengthening of faith is the most essential form of a Christian's effort at self-improvement. Strengthen your faith and you strengthen all graces; for it measures our reception of divine help.*[i]

It is impossible to live with the Supreme Savior unless we are diligent to develop this "established faith."

Finally, Paul says there must be an "abounding gratitude!" So imperative is the attitude of gratitude that it is impossible to live with the Supreme Savior until such has been developed. The person who walks with the Lord will be thankful for God's grace that does not punish according to what our sins deserve. There will be gratitude for the beauty of the earth which God designed for our enjoyment. There will be an overflowing of thanksgiving for the Lord's church and the blessed privilege we share in being members of it.

We are able to see the kind of devotion that is necessary if we are to live life with the Supreme Savior. It is firmly settled, ever growing, strong in stability, and unmatched in gratitude! Such devotion is worthy of the Supreme Savior alone. Let us be careful that we do not offer this deep devotion to anyone else.

THE DANGER

Paul is careful to let the brethren know that even though they are presently walking in Christ, there is grave danger ahead if they are not diligent (2:8). He cautions: "Take heed!" "Beware!" "Keep watch!" "Never relax!" The reason for this is the possibility that someone would "make spoil" of believers. This refers to the spoils of war, especially people who were carried off as slaves by the conquering army. It later came to refer to those who were "kidnapped," "seduced," or "led away." That such a danger is present today can be illustrated in many ways.

It has been quite common for the parents of college-age students to be interviewed in the media and tell how their child was led away by members of some religious cult. There have been hundreds of parents heartbroken because their child became the "spoil" of some fanatical cult. [Look again at the telephone call recounted in the introductory lesson.] Such is always tragic. The brethren in Colossae were faced with such a tragic possibility. If they followed the erring teachers and failed to give Christ the supremacy He deserved, they would become the "spoil" of error.

From verse 8 we are able to see the things which threatened the welfare of the Colossians. These same things offer a grave threat to believers in the Lord today and should be closely watched. *First, an empty philosophy can capture.* This is what Paul warned young Timothy about when he referred to *"knowledge which is falsely so called"* (1 Timothy 6:20). It parades around boasting of its great depth of learning.

The danger of philosophy is a great challenge in our day. Noted philosophers are acclaimed because of their denial of God. Much is discussed on evolution and noted philosophers are called to support that error. Our schools are filled with the philosophies which are "vain deceit." It must be remembered that vain philosophy and the Word of God have always been at odds (cf. 1 Corinthians 1:18-2:4). Let us be careful that we are not carried away by some "smooth talking" philosopher who has neither fear nor knowledge of Almighty God.

Second, the traditions of men will capture. As Christ was teaching and healing, a group of religious leaders approached Him asking upon what authority He acted (Matthew 21:23-27). In His reply, Christ points out that there are only two standards of authority—from MAN and from GOD. The two cannot be the same. In Colossae there were those who desired the authority of men rather than the authority of God. Paul's advice is to cast aside, as quickly as possible, the traditions of men. As Paul wrote to the Galatians, he was careful to impress them with the fact that his actions and words rested upon the authority of God, not men (see Galatians 1:1, 11, 12). Christ pointed out that those who follow the traditions of men participate in a "vain worship." Whenever we deal with traditions, we always hurt the feelings of some because they have failed to see the actions as traditions. There are those who will worship and practice certain acts simply because they are traditional. There are some who have become the captives of tradition by placing traditions as equally important as the Word of God.

Third, Paul says that we can become captives *by following the Old Testament laws*. The word "rudiments" can refer to a number of things. Some see here a reference to worship of the sun, moon, and stars. That such worship can capture and ensnare suspecting people is easily admitted. But it seems that here, as in Galatians 4:3, the word refers to the basic principles of the Mosaic system. These Laws were being bound on the Colossians. They were being told that they must follow certain portions of the Law. Paul simply says, "Do not become a captive to this old system which was done away."

There are those around us today who have fallen prey to this point. They seem to cherish the Old Testament laws more than they do the New Testament of Christ Jesus. We are told that we must observe the Sabbath and follow other "moral" laws in the Old Testament. There are those who honestly feel that all we need to do is to follow the Ten Commandments. A careful reading of Galatians 3 will bring to light in a forceful manner the simple truth which Paul states here—we have been freed from the old Law to serve under the New Law.

The only way for us to escape the danger found in verse 8 is to look at the word "after Christ." We must make sure that all we do is "after Christ" and not after man. It is so simple for us to take the same approach as the Colossian citizens did. We find it very tempting to "pick and choose" what to believe. If a doctrine suits our fancy, we will accept; but if we find it disagreeable, we will disregard it. But this approach to God's will is never possible if we follow "after Christ." Let us beware lest some clever teacher makes us captive to a system of thought that is opposed to Christ.

THE VICTORY

Those who live with the Supreme Savior will be participants in a glorious victory. Nothing can happen which will prevent us from sharing in this victory as long as we remain faithful to Christ. This fact should have been more than enough to persuade the Colossians to remain faithful to Christ.

From verses 9-15 we see the victory that is assured to all who live with the Supreme Savior. In verse 9 we find the grounds for this victory—Jesus Christ IS God! This verse is very emphatic in asserting the deity of Christ. There is nothing missing in Him that is not found in God. The very nature of God "dwells" [is a permanent part] of Christ. This thought has been discussed in detail as we looked at 1:19.

Because of His deity, we are assured of victory in the following areas. *There is victory in overcoming sin!* (vs. 9-13). Through Christ this victory is possible. Only God has the right to forgive sins, and He is willing to do so for those who obey Christ. *"I, even I, am the one who wipes out your transgressions for My own sake, and I will not remember your sins"* (Isaiah 43:25, NASV). The complete victory over sin is detailed by the following: In Christ we are completed; we are made full. In Christ we have truly repented and have thrown aside the old man of sin. In Christ we have life and an intimate relationship with God. This wonderful victory is only possible through obedience to Christ Jesus.

There is victory found in our freedom from the legal demands of the Law! (v. 14). The obligation to the Law is presented in the form of an I.O.U which cannot ever be paid. The NASV renders it as *"certificate of debt,"* and obligation to pay an amount which was impossible. But

Jesus Christ has blotted out the obligation. He has cancelled the debt. In Romans 8:1, 2 we read, *"There is therefore now no condemnation to them that are in Christ Jesus. For the law of the Spirit of life in Christ Jesus made me free from the law of sin and of death."* That is exactly what Paul is saying in verse 14. Christ has abolished the obligation which we were incapable of paying. In Romans 7 Paul goes to great length to show how the obligation of the Old Law no longer has bearing on our lives because of the glorious work of Christ Jesus. We today have victory over that law which was ineffective. We are able to serve under the freedom of grace found in Jesus Christ.

Finally, we have victory over all spiritual woes! (v. 15). The picture is of a conquering commander returning in a victory parade. His conquered slaves march before him, stripped of all power and pride. Such is what happened when Christ defeated all spiritual forces. His victory was not a small, insignificant event. He openly demonstrated *their inability* and *His great ability*. There is nothing in the material realm or the spiritual realm which can successfully challenge the great Commander.

It was this understanding which prodded Paul to write, "For I am persuaded, that neither death, nor life, nor angels, nor principalities, nor things present, nor things to come, nor powers, nor height, nor depth, nor any other creature, shall be able to separate us from the love of God, which is in Christ Jesus our Lord" (Romans 8:38, 39). I love to sing that hymn "Victory in Jesus" because it illustrates this point so well. Because Christ is God, and because Christ has "triumphed," there is no opposition that can overthrow God's divine purposes. When we live with the Supreme Savior, we will know this is a fact.

DRAWING IT ALL TOGETHER

As you look at death, do you have the same confidence that the dying captain possessed? If we are ever tempted to improve on the plans and designs of God, let us remember this paragraph in Colossians. *It stresses that we have Jesus and that is all we should want!*

Our blessed Lord has done everything for us. He wiped the slate clean and brought us a Law which is able to make us acceptable to our Heavenly Father. Our blessed Lord has offered us freedom and has promised us victory. But all of His offers are useless unless we are determined to live life with the Supreme Savior.

As you live life with the Supreme Savior, remember: The Beginning; The Devotion; The Danger; and most importantly, The Victory!

REFLECTIONS & RESOLUTIONS

Reflections from our study of Colossians 2:6-15:

1. Reflect on "receiving" Christ in verse 6b. What is the common view on this action? Look up other references in the Bible and see how the Scriptures use this term.

2. Reflect on the "walk" of verse 6b. Find other references in the book of Ephesians which discuss this walk. How should this walk be reflected in your life? Why is it important to "walk" in Christ?

3. Reflect on the danger in verse 8. How does this danger present itself today? Look at the three ways in which you may become a captive. Are these three ways still threatening? If so, how? Which of these three would pose the greatest threat (or presently poses a threat)?

4. Reflect on the victory in verse 15. Why should this be comforting to believers? How can we persuade others to find this victory? Is it possible that there are some in the Lord's church who do not know this victory? Look at the hymn "Victory in Jesus" and see how its thoughts parallel the text.

Resolutions arising from our study of Colossians 2:6-15:

1. Resolve that you will persuade others to "receive" Christ as Lord in the same way that Epaphras did with the Colossians.

2. Resolve that your life will be one that demonstrates clearly the "walk" with Christ.

3. Resolve that you will develop this "walk" by becoming rooted, built up, established, and overflowing with gratitude.

4. Resolve that you will find great comfort in the wonderful victory that is found in Christ Jesus.

---

[i] Lipscomb, David. A Commentary on the New Testament Epistles (Ephesians, Philippians, and Colossians). The Gospel Advocate Commentary Series, Vol. IV. Gospel Advocate Company, Nashville, TN. 1968, p. 275-276.

9

SUPPLANTING CHRIST'S SUPREMACY

"Let no man therefore judge you in meat, or in drink, or in respect of a feast day or a new moon or a sabbath day: which are a shadow of the things to come; but the body is Christ's. Let no man rob you of your prize by a voluntary humility and worshipping of the angels, dwelling in the things which he hath seen, vainly puffed up by his fleshly mind, and not holding fast the Head, from whom all the body, being supplied and knit together through the joints and bands, increaseth with the increase of God. If ye died with Christ from the rudiments of the world, why, as though living in the world, do ye subject yourselves to ordinances, Handle not, nor taste, nor touch (all which things are to perish with the using), after the precepts and doctrines of men? Which things have indeed a show of wisdom in will-worship, and humility, and severity to the body; but are not of any value against the indulgences of the flesh."
(Colossians 2:16-23)

Lord Chesterfield was on a mission in Brussels one time and was invited by Voltaire to have dinner with him at the house of an infidel woman. During the meal the conversation happened to turn to the affairs of England. "I think, my Lord," said Madame C., "the Parliament of England consists of five to six hundred of the best informed, and most sensible men in the kingdom." "True Madame, they are generally supposed to be so." "What then can be the reason that they tolerate so great an absurdity as the Christian religion?" "I suppose," replied his Lordship, "it is because they have not been able to establish anything better in its stead. When they do, I do not doubt that in their wisdom they will readily adopt it!"

There is no fact in the Bible as clear as the supremacy of Christ Jesus! He occupies a position which can be filled by none other. Because of His supreme position, He is referred to as the "Alpha"—the beginning, the very first. He is referred to as "the door." Just as the Ark had but one door through which safety could be gained, there is but one door by which our souls may find safety. As the "door" and the "alpha", His supremacy is unquestioned. This supremacy should never be misplaced or misdirected. If we allow it to be supplanted, we will forfeit the only way that eternal reward may be assured.

In the present passage, Paul deals with the heresy in Colossae. This grave threat was about to supplant the Savior's supremacy. From a careful reading of the text, it will be discovered that this threat was two-pronged. It was an enslaving legalism (vs. 16, 17), and it was a false mysticism (vs. 18, 19). The brethren at Colossae were being coerced into accepting these errors. Anyone who refused to accept these were burdened with guilt. I am sure that the advocates put on a great show of humility and asked those who refused to submit to these requirements, "HOW can you possibly be acceptable to God if you do not show your commitment by practicing these things?" When put like that, it was hard to refuse to practice these errors. Many had already given in and had submitted once again to these decrees (vs. 20, 21). This problem was grave and needed to be dealt with immediately. Paul takes special care to expose this error in very clear terms.

It is unfortunate that this danger is still threatening today. There are teachers who go about our country with some mystical, legalistic doctrine and by their great show of wisdom and empty humility they succeed in deluding thousands to follow them. Perhaps what is more amazing to notice is that there are thousands who are willing to place themselves under some legalistic system of "Do's" and "Don'ts." They willingly submit to burdens which are unreasonable. Therefore, the situation of Colossae is not removed from our modern era. We have those who seek to either add to God's system or to delete from it. By doing so, they have fallen prey to the danger addressed in our present text—they have supplanted the supremacy of the Savior! Careful attention must be given to this passage because it is most applicable to our modern times.

THE FOUR SUPPLANTERS

From the passage we are able to discover four things that could possibly be substituted for the supremacy of the Savior.

First, we discover that allegiance to the Old Testament system can supplant the Savior's supremacy (vs. 16, 17). Paul is clearly referring to the Old Testament in these verses. This is certain because of the words used. "Meat" refers to food in general. Leviticus 11 contains instruction about the regulations governing the food habits under the Old Testament system. "Drink" refers to the various regulations found in Leviticus 11:34 and Hebrews 9:10. The "Feast Days" denote the annual festivals of Israel: Passover, Atonement, etc. These are set forth in Leviticus 23. The "sabbath day" refers to the weekly Sabbath, the seventh day of the week (Exodus 20:11). "New Moons" were celebrated by those under the Old Testament by the blowing of horns and sacrifices (Numbers 10:10; 28:11; Nehemiah 10:33).

Paul is quick to point out that the believer in Jesus Christ has been FREED from these rules and regulations. Believers are free simply because the Old Law has been abolished; the requirements have been "blotted out" (Colossians 2:14). In writing to the Galatians, Paul deals with this same error. In Galatians 3:19-29 you will find one of the most comprehensive arguments in the Bible which shows that we are no longer bound by the Old Testament laws. In that passage Paul is careful to point out that the promise to Abraham was to be realized by faith and not by the law. Paul goes on then to show the purpose for the Law of Moses. Perhaps a fitting summary is found in verses 24 and 25, *"So that the law is become our tutor to bring us unto Christ, that we might be justified by faith. But now that faith is come, we are no longer under a tutor."*

The believers in Colossae had to be made aware of the fact that if they attempted to follow the Old Law, they would in effect be guilty of supplanting the supremacy of Christ Jesus. We must realize that same fact today. This does not mean that the Old Testament is no longer worthy of our study—it is! To the Romans Paul was careful to point out the merits of Old Testament study (Romans 15:4). Let us diligently study the Old Testament; but let us also understand that as we seek to know how we are to serve and worship God, we must look to the New Testament. Failure to recognize the Old Testament in the proper manner will result in the Savior being supplanted.

Second, we see that a false humility will cause Christ's supremacy to be supplanted (vs. 18a, 23). This humility is a pretense. It rests upon habits that are carefully cultivated instead of faith and love. Perhaps a good illustration is found in an incident which tells of a preacher's conversation with a member of the church where he preached. It seems that this member was in the habit of constantly going around saying, "What a poor, poor creature I am! I have fallen very short of God's expectations." Finally, having heard this far too many times, the minister replied, "You indeed have given me reason to believe that you are exactly as you say." Upon hearing that, the member angrily responded, "WHO told you anything about me? I am as good as you are? I will never come back to listen to you anymore! I will go somewhere else!" And he did.

We all know of people who make a great show of humility either by actions, dress, or show. This humility was being demonstrated in Colossae so that the false teachers could gain the sympathy and following of the unsuspecting members. Such devious intentions are visible by a number of people who are seeking to further their personal cause rather than the cause of Christ. They will parade themselves openly as a very pious and benevolent person; yet, if the truth should become known, it would reveal an inner heart that is both proud and arrogant. True humility does not have to be voiced. It is easily seen. And the truly humble persons are often totally unaware of their beautiful lives! Our brethren in Colossae were being confronted with those who professed to be pious and humble, but they were clever deceivers. Let us take heed and not be deceived by some "humble" teacher who is out to further his ways instead of God's.

Third, angel worship was supplanting Christ in Colossae (v. 18b). These false teachers prided themselves on being familiar with some spirit being. They claimed that this relationship gave their prayers an "edge" and they would receive answers much quicker than others. Instead of going directly to God through Christ, they were routing prayers and worship to God through angels. This error is fully condemned in the Bible (Revelation 19:10; 22:8, 9). Man is often tempted to place his trust in some kind of spirit being. Whenever this is done, the supremacy of Christ is immediately supplanted.

Fourth, visions can supplant Christ's supremacy (v. 18c). The false teachers prided themselves in the fact (?) that they were able to receive instructions directly from God through visions. I am sure that these visions would often command much more, or less, than the true revelations of God.

In our modern time there are many who claim that they have the "inside track" on God by being able to experience "visions." Immediately one thinks of Joseph Smith and the "visions" he received from the angel "Moroni." It is interesting to note that every new addition to Mormon theology has come as a result of "visions" received, either by Smith or by one of the "prophets" which succeeded him. As the Mormon church is carefully studied, it will become clear how great a danger the supplanter "Visions" is. Jesus Christ ceases to be the supreme Savior and more and more faith is placed on the visions or the modern prophet! The person who trusts in visions more than in the inspired revelations of God found only in the Bible, will be quickly caught in the snare of a mystical and emotional religion which is worthless! It is a sober fact that such visions may well be the working of Satan's power on those who are determined not to believe the Truth of God! (See 2 Thessalonians 2:9-12; 2 Corinthians 11:13-15).

THE IMPROPRIETY

Just as quickly as he told us what these supplanters were, the Apostle tells us why they are improper substitutes for our Lord's supremacy.

They are improper because they are based upon "men" and not God! (vs. 16, 18, 22). They command mere human ordinances, and not the divine ordinances of God. This type of ordinance is sternly rebuked by God in Isaiah 29:13 (NASV), *"Then the Lord said, 'Because this people draw near with their words and honor Me with their lip service, but they remove their hearts far from Me, and their reverence for Me consists of tradition learned by rote.'"* Following human rules will not make us acceptable to God. These commands based upon "men" were also unacceptable to God because they were based upon "a show of wisdom" (v. 23). Man's doctrine never possesses true wisdom because it does not rely upon God's wisdom. The impropriety of trusting in man's doctrine rather than in God's is clearly shown to the Colossians. They would be replacing Christ with man. They would be substituting the mediatorship of Christ with someone or something. They would be trusting in angels, dead spirits, or "inspired" leaders rather than in Christ who is the only way (cf. John 14:6). What a pitiful substitute!

They are improper because they are not the "substance" (v. 17). Paul clearly shows that the Mosaic Laws were never intended to make man perfect. They were made to bring us to Christ (Galatians 3:24). The Old Law was never intended to provide all things, just to show us in type what wonderful blessings would be found in Christ Jesus. But Christ is "the body"—He is the reality, the substance! In Him the blessings, promises, and hopes which the Old Law could only depict in a shadow, are a reality. Try to make the Old Testament, or angels, or inspired leaders provide and secure and solid foundation for spiritual blessings and you will face an impossibility.

They are improper because they fail to give the proper connection with the head (v. 19). If someone tries to add to the system of Christ, he will "lose his grasp" on the Savior. By substitution of the Lord's plans and pattern, one will actually sever himself from the head of Christ. Surely no one would want to cut themselves off from the head of Christ. If so, why should we try to add or delete from the divine plan of God?

THE TRAGIC CONSEQUENCES

Paul has now named the four supplanters and he has demonstrated why they are improper. Now we are able to see what dire consequences will result if the Colossians do not reject the supplanters.

First, life would be lived as though obedience to Christ had never been demonstrated (v. 20). They would still live as if they were in the world. The Apostle seems puzzled that the brethren would even think of submitting to these regulations again. Why do that when they have been freed by the blood of Christ? If we have obeyed our Lord's invitation, we need to model our lives after the spiritual rules of the New Testament.

Second, there will be the tragedy of "will-worship" (v. 23). This is a kind of worship that is self-imposed, self-made, self-directed, and self-invented. If we toss aside the supremacy of Christ and reject His authority for our lives, with what authority are we left? We will have only our own understanding to learn upon. However acceptable an addition may appear, or however "loving" a deletion may seem, such is folly at its height. It is simply labeled a "self-made religion." Those who are guilty of will-worship are basically saying, "God has not given us the complete system. Christ is not all-sufficient. We must add to it because WE know what is best!" Self becomes the guiding force.

A good illustration of how self will guide one in religious matters is found in Demetrius (Acts 19:23-27). He cried to the goddess Diana; yet it was not for her temple but her silver shrines that he so much adored! He was more in love with her wealth than with her worship. Listen to his word, *"Sirs, ye know that by this business we have our wealth."* The honesty of this silversmith is an excellent commentary on the entire scope of will-worshipers. They worship according to the dictates of "self," not God. They are more concerned with wealth than with true worship. How tragic it is to see those who base their faith upon visions and angels. They will soon find themselves in the terrible plight of making up their own religion.

Third, there will be the submission to requirements that are totally unnecessary (v. 21). The believers were constantly being told, "Don't," "Don't," "DON'T!" What a poor religion that always cried "Don't." It makes a person feel trapped and unable to even breathe for fear of transgressing some small command of man. This does not free the believer to do anything he wants. It places one under the obligation to always do that which pleases God. And he seeks to please God because he WANTS to do so, not because he HAS to do it (cf. Colossians 3:17).

Fourth, there will be absolute trust in worldly things (vs. 22, 23). How sad it is to see millions trusting in things that simply "perish with using." How often have we been guilty of expending vast amounts of time and energy upon things that "perish with using?" How many have gone to their eternal destiny having based that destiny on the hope of temporal things? When we substitute the supremacy of Christ for things of this world, we will be placing our eternal hopes on things which "perish with using!"

When Ptolemy built Pharos, he wanted his name placed upon it for all to see. But the architect, Sostratus, did not feel that the King (who paid only money) should get all of the credit while he (who designed and built it) received none. So, he put the King's name on the front in plaster; but underneath, in the eternal granite, he cut deeply his name, "Sostratus." The sea dashed against the plaster and chipped off bit by bit. It lasted the time of Ptolemy, but by and by the plaster was all chipped away and there stood the name "Sostratus." In much the same way, everything that man builds will slowly chip away, never lasting very long. But that which is written in granite will remain.

We can rest assured that God's works and His will are eternal and will never be chipped away. Knowing this we should seek those things which will last through the ages instead of those things which will only "perish with using." Not only does trust in worldly things emphasize the temporal, but it never gives any value for spiritual living (v. 23). The heart is never touched; the life is never made better; the victory over sin is never realized!

Fifth, there will be a robbery of our prize (v. 18). The word "rob" refers to an unjust judge or umpire who deliberately cheats and "throws the game." Paul assures us that if we allow the four supplanters to displace Christ, they will serve as the unfair judge and we will never receive the prize! We will be cheated out of the victorious crown of life (Revelation 2:10); the blessed mediatorship of Christ (1 Timothy 2:5); and, our eternal reward (1 Corinthians 3:8).

There is a tree called the "Manchineel" which grows in the West Indies. Its appearance is very attractive and its wood is beautiful. It bears a certain kind of fruit which resembles an apple. The fruit looks tempting and has a very fragrant smell. But to eat of this fruit means instant death. Its sap is so poisonous that if a few drops of it falls on the skin it will immediately blister and cause pain. The Indians used to dip their arrows into the juice so that when wounded the enemy would die. Such illustrates vividly the danger which faced our brethren in Colossae. They were being confronted with four things which looked appealing, yet each was deadly. If they left the security of the Supreme Savior, for any of the four, they would be "robbed" of their prize.

THE ENCOURAGEMENT

Having demonstrated the terrible calamity which comes from supplanting the Savior's supremacy, Paul gives his readers some points of encouragement which should strengthen them.

The Savior's supremacy frees us from guilt! We should not feel guilty because we are not following the teachings of Moses or the commands of some "inspired" leader. One has rendered verse 16 in this manner, "Do not let anyone take you to task?" Why? Because of the "therefore" in verse 16. We have died and are now living a life with the Supreme Savior (Colossians 2:6-15).

The Savior's supremacy eliminates the need for angels and visions! We do not need visions today because we have the complete, revealed will of God. This is found in the Bible (2 Peter 1:3). We do not need the assistance of angels as we approach God in prayer because we have "boldness" to enter into His very presence (Hebrews 10:19; 4:16). This is something which angels could NEVER provide! We do not need to serve angels because they are serving us. The Hebrew writer asks, *"Are they [angels] not ministering spirits, sent forth to do service for the sake of them that shall inherit salvation?"* (Hebrews 1:14).

The Savior's supremacy enables us to be partakers of the nature of God. "Whereby he hath granted unto us his precious and exceeding great promises; that through these ye may become partakers of the divine nature, having escaped from the corruption that is in the world by lust" (2 Peter 1:4). Why should we, or any believer, submit again to the ordinances which cannot offer us this great blessing?

The Savior's supremacy enables us to mature and grow into perfection. As we arrive at this perfection [maturity], we will see the folly and uselessness of these four substitutes (v. 19; cf. Ephesians 4: 15, 16). If believers will diligently study and mature in Christ, they will see the greatness of His supremacy and will never relinquish it to a substitute?

DRAWING IT ALL TOGETHER

What a pity it is that there are so many who are willing to supplant the supremacy of Christ with one of the four things found in our lesson text: The Old Testament System, False Humility; Worship of Spirit Beings; and Visions. Let us take close heed. Any addition to God's doctrine, no matter how innocent it may appear, is a serious error! All such additions will lead us away from Christ's supremacy. Our Lord does not need help from anything that we can possibly add to His pattern.

Let us be careful to cling to the supremacy of our Lord and Savior. When a shipwreck sailor, left to the mercy of the waves, has no help within reach except a piece of the mast which has survived the storm, he will cling to it every so closely! He will firmly grasp it with all his might. He will hold on to it as life itself. If a wave should toss him from it, he will swim with all his might to grasp it once again. To part with that plank is to perish, and so he clings ever so tightly. He has hold on the only possible hope of rescue and, therefore, will not let go! Such should be the case with believers today. Our only hope of rescue is the "Rock of Ages," the Lord Jesus Christ. The Christian possesses the Savior; he clasps Him; he cleaves to Him. Even though sin and the world seek to lessen his grasp, he knows that to part the Savior's presence is to perish. Therefore, with the resolve of Jacob, he says to Almighty God, "I will not let Thee go!" (Genesis 32:26).

"For freedom did Christ set us free:
Stand fast therefore,
And be not entangled again in a yoke of bondage"
(Galatians 5:1)

REFLECTIONS & RESOLUTIONS

Reflections from our study on Colossians 2:16-23:

1. Reflect on the four "supplanters" of Christ's supremacy. Why do some want to substitute these things for Christ? Of the four listed, which one do you think is the most dangerous? Why? Can you list other things that might be substituted for Christ's supremacy?

2. Reflect on the words of Isaiah 29:13. Why is "tradition" so important to some people? Why are there some who are willing to place tradition on equal authority with Scripture?

3. Reflect on Galatians 3. Carefully read this passage and outline Paul's argument showing that the Old Testament was never intended to save our souls. Be sure to look carefully and see how "faith" enables one to become a partaker of the promise made to Abraham.

4. Reflect on the tragic consequences which result as Christ is replaced. Which is the most disastrous? Why?

5. Reflect on the encouragement Paul gives us to remain steadfast in our faith. What does the word "judging" refer to in verse 16? Does this mean that no one can ever point out error and offer instruction for its correction? What other Scriptures support your answer?

Resolutions arising from our study on Colossians 2:16-23.

1. Resolve that you will be determined not to allow anything or anyone to supplant Christ's supremacy in your life.

2. Resolve that you will diligently study the Bible so that you can mature to the point where you can recognize "Supplanters" of Christ in life.

3. Resolve that you will cling to the Savior's supremacy and will never allow anything to lessen your grasp!

– 10 –
BRANDED BY THE SUPREME SAVIOR

"If then ye were raised together with Christ, seek the things that are above, where Christ is, seated on the right hand of God. Set your mind on the things that are above, not on the things that are upon the earth. For ye died, and your life is hid with Christ in God. When Christ, who is our life, shall be manifested, then shall ye also with him be manifested in glory."
(Colossians 3:1-4)

It is reported that a missionary to the African continent was so godly that as he travelled through the jungles visiting various villages the natives' drums announced his coming as, "Her comes the Jesus Christ man." Such a tribute reflects the point of the present lesson text. One who recognizes the supremacy of Christ will be marked so that all who come in contact with him will know immediately that here is a "Jesus Christ man!"

In the present paragraph we find Paul applying the doctrinal teachings of chapters one and two. The application is most practical to daily living. This is typical of Paul's writings. He often sets forth basic doctrines and then explains how these doctrines affect daily life (cf. Romans 12ff; Ephesians 4ff). Because of the great supremacy of Christ, every aspect of the believer's life should be affected.

From Colossians 3:1-4 we are able to see that there should be a noticeable change in our inward attitudes that is reflected in our outward behavior. In fact, believers who truly recognize Christ as the Supreme Savior will be "branded" in such a way that others will quickly know that they belong to the Lord. As Paul wrote to the Galatians (6:17) he mentioned that, *"I bear branded on my body the marks of Jesus."* Probably he was referring to physical scars which resulted from the many persecutions endured for his faith. But we can rest assured that had Paul never been beaten, he still would have been a "marked man" in the sense that his life was distinctively not his but the Lord's! Such an observation should lead us to look seriously at our lives. Are we bearing the brand-marks of Christ Jesus? Are others able to recognize that we are followers of Christ? From a careful study of this passage, we are able to see three "brand-marks" which every believer should wear. Look closed at each one and see if you are branded by the Supreme Savior.

YOU SHOULD BE BRANDED WITH...
A RESURRECTION (VS. 1A, 3A)

The Colossians had been the subject of a resurrection. The following points are discovered in connection with this resurrection.

First, THE ACTION—they were "raised." This is a clear reference to the immersion of 2:12. In immersion one obeys the will of God and has risen to walk a new life with God (cf. Romans 6:4). This raising is a spiritual resurrection; our sinful man was buried and left buried in the watery grave (Romans 6:6). It is simple, and should not need further comment; but notice that one can never be "raised" unless he is first "buried."

Second, THE REASON—death! The Colossians had "died" to the things of the world. In baptism that which is dead is buried. Whenever the Colossians died to the world, they were separated from the world (i.e., became "saints" of God). Because of this death, their past no longer held them captive.

I like the story that is often told to illustrate how in "dying" to the world there is a complete separation and entirely new life begins. Two young women once lived a very immoral life. These were known as the "life of the party" and were known to be willing to try "anything for kicks." These two came to know the glorious supremacy of Christ and put the Savior on by baptism. Shortly after their conversion, they received an invitation to attend a party. The invitation was "RSVP." Upon receiving it, they turned it over and wrote on the back, "Sorry we cannot attend . . . We have died!" These two women realized the wonderful point in our text and were willing to live as branded by Christ

Third, THE CONSEQUENCES—the resurrection of believers who put on Christ in baptism carries definite consequences. The word "IF" in verse 1 does not convey the sense of doubt, but a certain fact. Perhaps a word which would convey the certainty of this word would be "Since." By inserting this word, the phrase would read, "Since then ye were raised . . ." Their resurrection was a sure thing. Therefore, there were certain consequences which were to follow.

The means of this resurrection was the Colossian's immersion. It is amazing to consider how simple Paul understands this point but how complicated many denominational doctrines have made it. It is also interesting to read the remarks of many who hold leading positions in various denominations. These authors are almost in harmony in agreeing that this resurrection takes place in baptism. But they will contend that baptism is not necessary for salvation. Simple reason is permitted to ask, "IF it is necessary for one to be resurrected (in the sense found in the present text) in order to be saved, and IF baptism is that action by which one is raised, HOW can baptism *not* be important?" It is significant to note that Paul did not have to spend volumes arguing the necessity of immersion; he simply states it as a fact. The text is crystal clear—you do not follow the Supreme Savior, and you cannot be raised with Him until you have obeyed the command of baptism (cf. Colossians 2:12; 3:1)!

It should be evident to all you associate with that you have "died" and are now "risen" with the Lord Jesus Christ. Do you wear this brand-mark of the Supreme Savior?

YOU SHOULD BE BRANDED WITH ...
A MINDSET (VS. 1-2)

Perhaps this is the one point that is the hardest for most of us to demonstrate. The Colossians had changed their entire thought pattern! They had made a deliberate decision that they had to think as the Supreme Savior directed.

Elsewhere Paul tells us that we have the ability to decide what we think and how we think. As he wrote to the Philippians he noted, *"... Brethren, whatsoever things are true, whatsoever things are honorable, whatsoever things are just, whatsoever things are pure, whatsoever things are lovely, whatsoever things are of good report ...*

think on these things" (Philippians 4: 8, 9). Far too many believers think that they do not need to change their thought processes and try to live the Christian life with the same mindset as that which they lived with in the world. Let us remember that when we lived in the world, we were "alienated and enemies in your mind" (Colossians 1:21). To try to live the Christian life without changing your thoughts is to attempt an impossibility.

Further emphasis is found in the passage which helps us to see why we must develop this new mindset. We need to change our habit of thinking because: [1] Christ is "above." We need to set our thoughts on that which is precious to us. Being a follower of Christ, we must think on Him. [2} The things "above" are far greater than the things on the earth. That which is above is God-like and eternal in value. But that which is earthly is selfish, trivial, temporary, and, as Paul has earlier stated, will *"perish with using."* [3] Those who fail to change their mindset will never be able to enjoy the riches of heaven's rewards. In Philippians 3:17-21 Paul is careful to exhort the brethren at Philippi to walk in the right lifestyle. As he discusses those who walk in the wrong way, he lists traits which belong to those who are the *"enemies of the cross of Christ: whose end is perdition."* Listen to the traits mentioned by Paul: their god is the belly, their glory is in shame, and *they mind earthly things*! We must change our mindset so that we will be able to enter into heaven.

This does not mean that we are to be unconcerned and indifferent about the things of the earth. Paul is saying that as followers of the Supreme Savior, we are not to allow life on earth to become our "god." We should look at this world from a heavenly viewpoint. [4] Those who develop this mindset will possess proper focusing. We see that the spiritual outweighs the material. We will be able to see the proper devotion that is due to God and will not try to render a divided affection. We will focus on the great devotion of the Psalmist, *"As the deer pants for the water brooks, so my soul pants for You, O God. My soul thirsts for God, for the living God"* (42:1, 2, NASV). This ability to focus will cause us to "hunger and thirst after righteousness (Matthew 5:6)."

In the lesson text, Paul is careful to show us that this mindset must be earnestly developed. It is never easy to change the way you think; especially is this true regarding spiritual matters. Our present society discourages the mindset which follows the Savior's Supremacy.

Anselm illustrated the great need to guard our thoughts with the following story. Our heart is like a mill, ever grinding, which a lord gave in charge to his servant, enjoining that he should only grind in it his master's grain, whether wheat, barley, or oats, and telling him that he must subsist on the produce. But that servant has an enemy who is always playing tricks on the mill. If, any moment, he finds it unwatched, he throws in gravel to keep the stones from acting, or pitch to clog them, or dirt or chaff to mix with the meal. If the servant is careful in tending his mill, there flows forth a beautiful flour, which is at once a service to his master, and subsistence to himself; but if he plays the truant, and allows his enemy to tamper with the machinery, the bad outcome tells the tale; his lord is angry; and he himself is starved! This mill, ever grinding is the mind; thoughts are the grain; the Devil is the watchful enemy. The Devil throws in bad thoughts, which can only be prevented by watchfulness and prayer.

To keep our minds centered on the Savior's supremacy, Paul says that we must develop this mindset from two perspectives. *First*, it must be developed from an outward perspective—"seek" ["keep seeking," NASV]. This command has to do with our visible deeds. We must show energy in actions. We must demonstrate that we possess this mindset of Christ's supremacy. *Second*, it must be developed from an inward perspective— "set your mind." This command refers to our attitudes. One can perform pious deeds but lack the essential attitude. But when we follow the Supreme Savior, we will show efforts (seek) and possess attitudes (fix the mind) on the things that are above.

Whenever one is branded by this mindset, his thoughts, attitudes, and deeds will be seen by all as arising from his relationship with Christ Jesus. Do you bear this brand-mark of the Savior's Supremacy?

YOU WILL BE BRANDED WITH...
A SECURITY (VS. 3B-4)

In the closing verses of this section, we find confident security expressed by Paul. The Colossians were secure because they had been "hid with Christ." This same assurance is found elsewhere in the Bible. It is Stephen standing calmly in the midst of his murderers and saying, "*Behold, I see the heavens opened, and the Son of Man standing on the right hand of God" (Acts 7:56).* It is Job sitting in the dust, covered with sores and saying, "*I know that my Redeemer liveth*" (Job 19:25a), and "*Though He slay me, yet will I trust in Him*" (Job 13:15, KJV). It is Peter declaring before the council, "*This is the stone which was set at nought of you builders, which is become the head of the corner. Neither is there salvation in any other: for there is none other name under heaven given among men, whereby we must be saved*" (Acts 4:11, 12, KJV). This security is wonderfully summed up in the confident challenge, "*Who shall lay anything to the charge of God's elect? It is he that justifieth?*" (Romans 8:33). Security fostered by the Savior is found in the aged prisoner's words, "I know whom I have believed..." (1 Timothy 1:12b) and "There is a crown laid up for me" (2 Timothy 4:8b). Our lives on earth may be filled with weakness, sickness, pain, trying and anxious moments, but security offered by the Savior is more than this life. It is health, strength, power, vigor, activity, energy, and beauty!

Thus, when Paul affirms that the Colossians, and all believers, are "hid with Christ," he is expressing the assurance that is a blessed security. Perhaps one passage which expresses the believer's security clearest is found in John 10:27-29, "*My sheep hear my voice, and I know them, and they follow me: and I give unto them eternal life; and they shall never perish, and no one shall snatch them out of my hand. My Father who hath given them unto me, is greater than all; and no one is able to snatch them out of the Father's hand.*" This text is a wonderful commentary on our present text. The Colossians had heard the voice of Christ and followed the Lord's will as the gospel was preached. Because of this they were "hid with Christ" and would remain secure as long as they continued in His will.

Some try to distort this concept of security by asserting that one who is saved is never going to sin to an extent that he will be eternally lost. Such cannot be true when it is remembered that the main purpose for the writing of the Colossian letter was to prevent the believers there from falling away from Christ. If the Colossians had been "hid" to an extent that they would enjoy eternal life and security from apostasy, this epistle would have never been necessary! Surely the reason and logic of Scripture is able to outweigh such weak doctrines of human origin.

From the closing verses in this section, we are able to see three facts which combine to provide this security. *First,* as already mentioned, we are "hid with Christ." *Second*, we are secure because Christ is our "life." He gives meaning to life. He gives the force and strength that is necessary for life (John 14:6; 1 John 5:11; Galatians 2:20). *Third,* we are secure because of our prospect for the future— "GLORY!" Christ is sitting at the right hand of God and He will come back to claim His own.

How do you anticipate His second coming? Is it a time of joy? Apprehension? Fear? To the believer it is a time of confident expectation. We should be able to look ahead to that day with great joy. "... *My little children, abide in him; that, if he shall be manifested, we may have boldness, and not be ashamed before him at his coming"* (1 John 2:28). Carefully read 1 Thessalonians 4:13-18 and see the joyful expectation that should characterize believers in the second coming. Carefully notice that Paul says, "When" and not "If" Christ comes back. His coming is a certain thing and we should find great security in it. One other thought—Paul speaks of this as a *"blessed hope"* (Titus 2:13). Is His return a blessed hope to you? It is if you are following the Supreme Savior.

DRAWING IT ALL TOGETHER

The Christian must be different from those who are in the world. As a follower of the Supreme Savior, others should be able to look at your attitudes and actions and say, "There is the Jesus Christ man!" This recognition will result only by our being branded by the Supreme Savior.

We have seen that the Savior marks His followers with three brand-marks. He brands us with a resurrection through baptism. He brands us with a mindset that is firmly fixed and constantly seeking the things above. He brands us with a security that is not to be found anywhere else.

Are you branded by the Supreme Savior? Look carefully at these three points and personally apply them to our life.

REFLECTIONS & RESOLUTIONS

Reflections from our study of Colossians 3:1-4:

1. Reflect on the point that the "brand-marks" of the Savior are visible to others around us. How are they visible? List some "brand-marks" which may be added to those in this lesson.

2. Reflect on how baptism is a "resurrection." What other texts in the Bible refer to baptism in this way? Since baptism is the manner in which we are "raised with Christ," why do some say it is not necessary? List some other reasons which show the essentiality of baptism.

3. Reflect on how our "death" changes our lives. List some areas where this change should take place. Have you ever known of some who were like the two young women mentioned in the lesson whose life with the Savior was a drastic change?

4. Reflect on the necessity of changing your mindset. What other passages emphasize the need to guard and protect our thoughts? Why is this often the hardest thing to do?

5. Reflect on the security found in Christ. Do you think that most members of the church share this feeling of security? Why? What often hinders one from knowing

this security? Look carefully at John 10:27-29 and see how these words of Jesus compare with the words of Paul. Why do you think some hold a misconception of John 20:27-29? From a study of this verse, list two things that are essential if security is to be present in the believer's life.

Resolutions arising from our study on Colossians 3:1-4:

1. Resolve that you will be known as one who bears the brand-marks of the Supreme Savior.

2. Resolve that you will carefully consider the three brand-marks discussed in this lesson and make sure they are in your life.

= 11 =
THE PAST IS NOT PRESENT WITH THE SAVIOR

"Put to death therefore your members which are upon the earth: fornication, uncleanness, passion, evil desire, and covetousness, which is idolatry; for which things' sake cometh the wrath of God upon the sons of disobedience: wherein ye also once walked, when ye lived in these things; but now do ye also put them all away: anger, wrath, malice, railing, shameful speaking out of your mouth: lie not one to another; seeing that ye have put off the old man with his doings, and have put on the new man, that is being renewed unto knowledge after the image of him that created him: where there cannot be Greek and Jew, circumcision and uncircumcision, barbarian, Scythian, bondman, freeman:
but Christ is all, and in all."
(Colossians 3:5-11)

The immortal words of John Newton's hymn serve well to echo the lesson contained in the present paragraph—"I once was lost, but now am found; was blind but now I see."

From these words we are able to see the understanding of the believer who has the balanced outlook between the past, the present, and the future. It is only through the "amazing grace" of God that Christians are able to look at the past so confidently assured of the present.

From the present paragraph, we are able to discover a very wonderful lesson. Because of the Savior's supremacy, our past IS NOT present. There has been a drastic change in practice and position. Because the Colossians had submitted to the Supreme Savior, there was a definite contrast evident in their personal lives. This contrast was present only because they chose to cooperate with the commands of Christ Jesus.

The practical aspect of this present text is easily seen. A studied look at members in the Lord's church will reveal three large groups. There are those members who once lived a life devoted to the world. They committed many "great and grave" sins which still burden them with a constant load of guilt. They do not feel comfortable in accepting the fact that the Lord has forgiven them of their past sins completely. To this group, the present section says, "Do not bind yourselves with guilt. The past has been dealt with; it is forever removed and has no bearing at all on your present life!"

There is a group of members who have no yet seen the necessity of severing all worldly practices and habits from their lives. They continue to do some of the things that they did before they obeyed the gospel. To this group the present text says, "Do not fool yourself! You must put to death; you must put them ALL away!"

And then there is that group which has seen the necessity of completely severing themselves from the past. They have tried repeatedly and failed to overcome some besetting sin in their lives. Because of this constant failure, they are depressed, distressed, and about to give up. They feel terrible because it seems that they are always going to God to ask Him to forgive them for the same sin. To this group the text says, "Do not give up! Keep trying, even if such efforts appear to be dismal failures. Keep trying because you are being renovated by God's knowledge and you will one day succeed. You must keep up the fight!"

Each reader should be able to place himself into each of these groups. As you do, you should find that practicality of this marvelous passage. As the paragraph is closely considered, it will be observed that Paul brings three different looks to our attention. We discover a sober look at the past, a relieved look at the Savior's actions, and a thankful look at our present position in life.

A SOBER LOOK AT THE PAST

Paul carefully shows his readers what their past life was like. In these verses there is an honest description of what one is like when he is outside of Christ. Notice five traits of the past which are common to all who are outside of Christ's salvation.

First, we all were once devoted to earthly passions (3:5, 6a). Five sins are mentioned by Paul to show us how we were once dominated by the sinful desires of the world.

"Fornication" is a word which can refer to any sexual immortality. It comes from the Greek word *PORNEIA*, from which we get our English word "pornography." Whatever is included in "pornography" is included in the word used by Paul here. "Uncleanness" refers to any act, word, or thought that is unworthy of the nature of Christ. This word is used by Paul in Romans 1:24 to refer to sexual perversion.

"Passion" refers to the emotion or feeling that enslaves a person's mind. Again, this is used by Paul in Romans 1:26, 27 as he discusses the Gentiles' sinful condition without Christ or the Law.

"Evil desires" are the thoughts and desires which prod men toward the forbidden things in the world. Such desires are wrong because sooner or later they will gain the upper hand in a person's life and will dictate actions.

"Covetousness" refers to a greedy desire for more and more. This evil does not take into consideration the rights of others or the decrees of God. The covetous person will use unfair advantage to obtain the object desired. This sin is the root of all other sins. It is a man's greed that fosters every sin and carries out sin. Knowing this, our Lord warned, *"Take heed, and keep yourself from all covetousness: for a man's life consisteth not in the abundance of things which he possesseth* (Luke 12:15b). It is amazing to consider, but I do not ever recollect hearing anyone confess guilt of this sin. Covetousness has been called the "unmentionable sin" and perhaps this is a good title for it. The Colossians had been guilty of these sins in their past. They had recognized them as sin and had repented of them. Let us take careful thought of their danger and sever ourselves from them as well.

Second, we lived in association with disobedience (3:6c). We surrounded ourselves with those who were "sons of disobedience." Our very best friends defied God. Our lives were designed with God's absence. Because of our association, we too were identified with these "sons of disobedience."

Third, we had a lifestyle which was dedicated to error (3:7). Not only had the Colossians been associated with people who demonstrated the five sins above, but they had actually lived a life doing these things. As Paul wrote the Corinthians (1 Corinthians 6:9ff), he reminded them of their past. He mentions that once they were fornicators, idolators, homosexuals, thieves, covetous, drunkards, revilers, and extortioners, and then writes,

"*And such were some of you.*" The Colossians and Corinthians had practiced these habits on a daily basis. Their lifestyles were opposed to God. Although many of us refuse to admit it, we were exactly like these first century brethren. Now, our lives may not have been as caught up in the same immoralities as these were, but we were still living a life that was contrary to the will of God. We were guilty of living in the manner that Paul describes, "*...Ye once walked according to the course of the world, according to the prince of the powers of the air, of the spirit that now worketh in the sons of disobedience*" (Ephesians 2:2). Do you remember when your past was like this?

Fourth, we demonstrated a complete lack of self-control (3:8, 9a). From the passage, we see five sins that are named by Paul. Each of these five are present in the life of the one who has failed to master self-control. Anger, wrath, malice, railing, and shameful speaking are all consequences of a missing self-control. The frightening thought that is discovered from this verse is—here are sins that most of us have grown accustomed to in life. So accustomed are we to anger that when it is displayed, we do not see the need to rebuke its presence. We try to excuse and rationalize each one of these sins instead of developing the self-control that is demanded by God. The believer has absolutely NO BUSINESS associating with those who demonstrate these evil habits. "*Putting away therefore all wickedness, and all guile, and hypocrisies, and envies, and all evil speakings . . . that ye may grow thereby unto salvation*" (1 Peter 2: 1, 2). The self-control that will govern these five sins is found only when the Savior's supremacy has been accepted and followed in life. Can you remember when your life was characterized by these sins?

Fifth, we had the wrath of God to look forward to in the Judgment and in eternity (3:6b). God's wrath is a serious part of His nature and one is a fool to take it lightly. *"Let no man deceive you with empty words: for because of these things cometh the wrath of God upon the sons of disobedience* (Ephesians 5:6). If we had continued in this kind of lifestyle, which does not fear God and keep His commands, we would have had to stand and face His terrible wrath on the Judgment Day!

Now, this is exactly how the Colossians looked when they were apart from the Supreme Savior. And this is a sober look at what our past once looked like. We were reprobates. We were incapable of doing anything on our own to merit salvation. It is good for each of us to cast a backward glance and remember just how terrible we once were. But we do not stop with this sober look at our past because now Paul brings us to…

A RELIEVED LOOK AT HOW THE SAVIOR'S SUPREMACY CHANGED OUR PAST

The fact that change took place is evident as Paul uses the opening words of verse 8, "but now . . ." Change was evident in the Colossians. But how did this change take place? The answer is found in verse 10. By "knowledge" we learned what our spiritual condition was and what we needed to do to respond to God's will. This knowledge is what Epaphras taught the Colossians (cf. Colossians 1:6b, 7, 9, 10). It is through this knowledge that we are able to live godly lives. As Paul instructed Titus concerning duties on Crete, he reminded Titus that the knowledge of God's truth will lead the Cretans to live godly lives (Titus 1:1b).

It is through this knowledge that our hearts are changed and we desire to serve God fully. The Psalmist prayed, *"Create in me a clean heart, O God, and renew a steadfast spirit within me"* (51:1, NASV). Whenever a person comes to the proper knowledge of God's will, there must be change present. The power of God's Book to change character is universally admitted. Even those who deny the Bible's inspired truth about the immortal soul will admit its power to mold character.

An English barrister who was accustomed to training students in the practice of the Law, and who was not himself a religious man, was once asked why he put students, from the very first, to the study and analysis of the most difficult parts of Scripture. "Because," he said, "there is nothing else like it, in any language, for the development of mind and character." Through the "knowledge of God's Word our past sins will find forgiveness, and we will demonstrate a truly changed life.

Further examination of this passage will reveal just *how* this knowledge leads to change in our lives.

First, this knowledge leads us to a DECISION. We decide to "put to death" and to "put all way." This "putting to death" is an interesting point to consider. It should be viewed from two aspects—there is a once-for-all putting away, and there is a constant day-by-day putting away. In the text Paul reminds the Colossians that they have "put to death." The verb tense refers to a decision that is made and does not ever have to be made again. The decision refers to a resolve that they will no longer be subjects of sin. They have once-for-all decided that their subjection to sin is over!

Other references which reflect this once-for-all decision are found in Romans 6:11 where believers should reckon themselves "to be dead unto sin." Again, in the Galatian epistle (5:24), believers *"have crucified the flesh with the passions and the lusts thereof."* But there is a daily struggle with sin. As we face each day, we will encounter temptations which must be "put to death." This day-by-day struggle is referred to in Romans 8:13, *"For if you are living according to the flesh, you must die; but if by the Spirit you are putting to death the deeds of the body, you will live"* [NASV]. The very tense used denotes a continuous action that results from past decisions. Believers have once-for-all decided to follow the Savior's supremacy in their lives; therefore, they are obligated to day-by-day put to death the desires and affections that are opposed to God. This decision is not easy, but it is right! The word "death" suggests that there will be a struggle, pain, and agony involved in living according to God's standards.

Second, after God's knowledge had led to a decision on our part, there will be ACTIONS. Paul says that we "put off" and "put on." This action is only accomplished by baptism into Christ for the forgiveness of sins. The fact that our past was "put off" at baptism is verified in Romans 6:6, *"Knowing this, that our old man was crucified with him, that the body of sin might be done away, that so we should no longer be in bondage to sin."* The fact that it is in baptism that we "put on" Christ is easily seen by reading Galatians 3:27, *"For as many of you as were baptized into Christ did put on Christ."* So clear is the Apostle's stress on the importance of baptism that it is amazing to see many refuse to admit its importance.

An irreligious merchant had been absent from his store for some time, and on his return noticed a marked change in one of his clerks. He said to his partner, "I do not understand what has come over George. He doesn't seem like the same person he once was. He seems changed since I went away. He was always smart, but now he seems more tender, respectful, and genial." The partner answered, "I suppose you know what has happened to him since you have been gone?" "I don't know what you are referring to." The answer came, "George has become a Christian." Whenever one comes to the "knowledge" of God's Word, change will occur. This change will come as a result of a decision that prompts actions.

Our sober look at the past has led to a relieved look at how the Savior's supremacy changed the past. Now Paul focuses our attention on . . .

A THANKFUL LOOK AT THE PRESENT

The emphasis of Paul in this passage is upon our present condition. The Christian's greatest concern is with the "NOW," not with the "THEN." Now he is liberated from sin. Now he is in Christ. Now he is acceptable to God. Now he must exhibit an entirely different attitude toward sin and toward those who are the "sons of disobedience." Now he is a new creature in Christ. Now, because of the Savior's supremacy, he can never be the same person he once was.

There is a great contrast drawn by Paul in this text. It is good to consider this contrast. We have looked soberly at the past, but do we look thankfully at the present?

We can be thankful because we are being "renewed." The New American Standard Version has a footnote to this word which reads "renovated." God is "Remodeling" us for His purposes. We are being ever so slowly changed and will one day be that which God desires. Paul understood this point and he referred to it in 2 Corinthians 4:16, "*Wherefore we faint not; but though our outward man is decaying, yet our inward man is renewed [renovated] day by day."* This renovation is a long, slow process that is accomplished only as the Word of God directs our lives and attitudes (cf. Romans 12:1, 2). This process is never ending. We will always be constantly changing, constantly removing, constantly remodeling! My children sing a song which epitomizes the Apostle's words here...

> "He's still working on me,
>   To make me what I ought to be.
> It only took a week to make the moon and stars,
>   The Sun and Earth and Jupiter and Mars.
> Oh! How patient He must be—
> He's still working on me!"

This renovation is in direct contrast to the devotion to earthly passions (vs. 5, 6a) and to the lack of self-control (vs. 8, 9a).

We can be thankful because now we share in a beautiful fellowship (v. 11a). In the Lord's church there is universal equality among all believers—none is greater than any other. Because of our brotherhood, all members are united with each other (Galatians 3:28). This fellowship is in direct contrast with the fellowship shared "then" (v. 6c). Previously we were in fellowship with the "sons of disobedience," but now we are in fellowship with the "saints of God." This fellowship shared now is one that is lacking the barriers which prejudice holds (v. 11a). In fact, it is impossible for those in Christ to carry the prejudicial barriers which exist in the world. These have been put all away.

We can be thankful now because we trust Christ as everything (v. 11). "Then" we trusted ourselves and those who were our associates in the world. But "now" we realize that Christ is ALL. We know the futility of trying to live according to the lifestyle of the world (vs. 6c, 7). Christ is ALL we need.

"Jesus is all the world to me,
My life, my joy l, my all;
He is my strength from day to day—
Without Him I would fall."

We can be thankful because now we have the hope of eternal glory (v. 11b). Since Christ is all in our lives, we will follow His will. As we follow His will, we will be reconciled through His death unto God (Colossians 1:22). In being reconciled, we will look to Him for life and long for His coming so that we will be forever with Him in glory (Colossians 3:4). Our present position is in direct contrast with how we were "then"—anticipating only the wrath of God (v. 6b).

Perhaps the following chart will help us firmly fix in our minds this great contrast that is presented by Paul.

"THEN"	"NOW"
Devoted to earthly passion (5, 6a)	Being renovated (10)
Lived with disobedience (6c)	Beautiful Fellowship (11a)
Life devoted to error (7)	Christ is our ALL (11)
Lacked self-control (8, 9a)	Renovation! (10)
Wrath of God awaiting us (6b)	We have the hope of glory (11b)

Surely, we are able to see by this contrast our past IS NOT present when we are following the Supreme Savior! Because of Christ, we have a thankful look at our present spiritual state.

DRAWING IT ALL TOGETHER

Are you able to see how the Supreme Savior changes life in such a wonderful way? He can fill it with joy and hope. He can offer complete pardon for all of the wrongs that you have ever committed. He can free you from the tragic destiny that the past assures.

Look once again to the three groups that this section speaks to. To those who are struggling with guilt, remember the Savior's supremacy. He has forgiven you of all past sins! There is nothing you can do about the past. Learn to trust confidently in the Savior's supremacy and forgiveness. To those who are struggling with a besetting sin, remember the Savior's remodeling program! He is still working on you. He is renovating and redesigning you by His Word. Be sure to study His Word and allow it to help you decide life's decisions. To those who have not severed association with sin, remember the decision which obliges you to "put to death" and to "put them ALL away." You cannot continue in sin and serve the Supreme Savior.

Remember the three looks which we have discovered in this passage: The Sober Look, The Relieved Look, and The Thankful Look!

REFLECTIONS & RESOLUTIONS

Reflections from our study on Colossians 3:5-11:

1. Reflect on the three groups of church members mentioned in this lesson. Look carefully at the lesson text and write out some advice you would offer to each group.
   a. To those who bind themselves with guilt over the past.
   b. To those who try to hold onto God and to sins.
   c. To those who try to overcome a besetting sin but constantly fail.
2. Reflect on the "sober look" of the past. Why is it good for one to remember how he/she was in the past? Which of the five traits mentioned do you think is the worst?
3. Reflect on the "relieved look." Where else in Colossians do you read of the Savior's effect on our present condition? Do you think most members share this relieved look in common? Why
4. Reflect on the two ways of "putting sin to death." Can you think of an illustration which will help explain the difference? Why is it necessary for us to "put to death" on a daily basis?
5. Reflect on the "thankful look." Which of the contrasts is the most impressive to you? Why? How does the fact that we are being "renewed" [renovated] offer encouragement to believers?

Resolutions arising from our study on Colossians 3:5-11.

1. Resolve that you will express constant thanksgiving to God because of what you were like in the past but are now like in the present. All has changed because of His grace.

2. Resolve that you will diligently study God's Word so that your "renovation" will be carried out in the best way.

~ 12 ~

SUPREMACY'S VISIBILITY

"Put on therefore, as God's elect, holy, and beloved, a heart of compassion, kindness, lowliness, meekness, longsuffering; forbearing one another, and forgiving each other, if any man have a complaint against any; even as the Lord forgave you, so also do ye: and above all these things put on love, which is the bond of perfectness. And let the peace of Christ rule in your hearts, to the which also ye were called in one body; and be ye thankful. Let the word of Christ dwell in you richly; in all wisdom teaching and admonishing one another with psalms and hymns and spiritual songs, singing with grace in your hearts unto God. And whatsoever ye do, in word or in deed, do all in the name of the Lord Jesus, giving thanks to God the Father through him."
(Colossians 3:12-17)

Two men were traveling on the western frontier. One of them took every occasion to declare Christianity as a delusion; and its professors, hypocrites. He stated that he always took special care of his valuables when with a Christian. As night was coming on, they sought shelter at the cabin of a poor settler and were welcomed to the best that the place afforded. The suspicion of the travelers became aroused; this cordiality might be intended to deceive them, and the loneliness of the place seemed to invited deeds of darkness. They resolved to take special precaution against surprise, to have their weapons ready; and one was to watch as the other slept. Before retiring to rest, the host, an old man, took down a well-worn Bible, read a portion, then prayed, asking that the strangers might have prosperity on their journey, and when their earthly journey should end, that they might have a home in heaven. Retired to their room, the skeptic, who had the first watch, instead of priming his pistol, prepared for sleep. His companion reminded him of their earlier arrangement. The infidel confessed that he could feel just as safe where the Bible was read and prayers offered as they had just heard, as at a New England fireside.

This incident serves to illustrate the thrust of our present text. The old man was careful to make sure that Christ's supremacy was visible in his life. Because of this visibility, there was a sure confidence placed in him by the travelers.

Within the text we find an implied "ought." Having acknowledged the Savior's Supremacy, we *ought* to make sure it is visible in our lives. As Paul discussed the results of obedience in Romans 6:4, he observed that as we rise from the watery grave of baptism, we have died "*so we also might walk in newness of life.*" It is this "newness of life" that is the visible demonstration of the Savior's supremacy in our lives. In the closing chapters of Colossians, Paul is concerned about his readers understanding the practical side of doctrine. Paul tells us that the doctrine in chapters one and two must influence daily living if it is valid. You and I cannot acquire an intelligent understanding of God's principles and be content with no more. Knowledge and understand must lead to a daily demonstration.

Since the Colossians were risen with Christ, they have new standards. They possess an entirely new life. They have easily discarded some things; but they have had to "put to death" other things. As they "put off," "put away," and "put to death," there was a void created in their lives, and that void must be filled. There is a common law of nature that states any void will be filled and this same law applies to spiritual things. We must immediately fill the void created in "putting off" or our condition could become worse than before.

To illustrate this somber point, our Lord told of one who had a demon cast out. The demon wandered around seeking a refuge but found none. Finally, the demon decided to go back to the one he had possessed. As the demon went back, he found that his "old home" had been "swept and garnished. *"Then goeth he, and taketh to him seven other spirits more evil than himself; and they enter in and dwell there: and the last state of that man becometh worse than the first"* (Luke 11:26).

Paul tells his readers that they must fill this void immediately or they will fall into a terrible calamity. As we study this paragraph, we discover that as the spiritual void is filled the Savior's supremacy will become very visible in daily living. Three ways in which this visibility is demonstrated can be found in these verses.

THE SAVIOR'S SUPREMACY WILL BECOME VISIBLE BY...
A DISTINCTIVE LIFESTYLE (VS. 12A, 17)

The rationale for this lifestyle is found. Why should we make our lives distinctive? Why should we go to the trouble, pain, and toil of "putting to death?" Paul's answer is simple. He says we have been "chosen." We are the "elect" of God! Because of this simple fact, we read, "Therefore." We have put off; we have put to death; we have put all away—THEREFORE it is reasonable that we do this. *"For ye were once darkness, but are now light in the Lord; walk as children of light"* (Ephesians 5:8).

This election is further described in 1 Peter 2: 9, 10. Ephesians 1:4 shows us how we were chosen by God. By our submission to His will, we were placed "in Christ." Those who are found "in Christ" are those who have been chosen, or elected, by God to eternal life. Our choosing to follow the commands of God resulted in God's choosing us to be His children. This election is not an individual election but a group election. Those who are in Christ (in the group of His believers and faithful followers), have become the recipients of His grace and mercy. Because we are children, we must live a distinctive lifestyle. This is the reasonable thing to do!

The character of this lifestyle is discussed. It is "holy." This refers to two broad areas. Our practice of living is such that it becomes holy, set apart as a devoted service to Almighty God. Our attitudes and thoughts have become holy. We have set our minds on the things above, and this has affected our entire thought pattern.

This lifestyle is also "devoted." From verse 17 we are able to see that this life encompasses ALL that we do in both word and deed. Such a lifestyle is truly devoted to the service of the Savior.

This lifestyle is also "guarded." Once again, notice that in verse 17, Paul says that our lives will be guarded by the Savior's name. The presence of the Lord's name will guard our lives and preserve the purity of our Christian character. One of the best tests to gauge your conduct by is to ask, "Can I do this in the name of the Lord Jesus Christ?"

There should be nothing in our lives which has escaped this litmus test of the Savior's supremacy. "*...Let every one that nameth the name of the Lord depart from unrighteousness*" (2 Timothy 2:19b). Everything we do must be related to His blessed name. Do you see how such an understanding will "guard" our Christian character? Brother David Lipscomb remarked, "If he is to do everything in Christ's name, he must do nothing with which he cannot associate it."[ii] Take a close look at the words of the hymn "Take the Name of Jesus with You," and see how the words of this song express the same guarded protection which Paul commands in verse 17.

The reward of this distinctive lifestyle is revealed. We become those who are "beloved of God." This great love has no limits. One of man's basic needs is to know that he is loved. By living this distinctive lifestyle, God has shown us that we will be rewarded with a love that is matchless. What greater reward could there be?

THE SAVIOR'S SUPREMACY WILL BECOME VISIBLE BY...
CLOTHING YOURSELF WITH GODLY GARMENTS (VS. 12B-15)

Consider *the action* commanded— "put on!" The verb is imperative and describes an action which must be carried out without any delay or hesitation. Remember, hesitation to fill the void will result in dire consequences. The ancient patriarch Job remarked, *"I put on righteousness, and it clothed me; my justice was like a robe and a turban* (Job 29:14, NASV). Have you "put on" the godly garments that are described in this section?

Consider *the reason* we are to put on these godly garments. We have just mentioned it. We are God's elect, holy, and beloved! What greater reason can there be?

Closely *consider the wardrobe* which Christians must put on. There is "compassion." This is the ability to put ourselves "in the shoes" of others. We are able to feel their joys and sorrows, their peaks and pains through life. We are able to *"Rejoice with those who rejoice, and weep with those who weep*" (Romans 12:15, NASV). One of the other versions [NLT] renders this as "tenderhearted mercy." Because of this, our hearts are softened and our judgment is lessened. This ability was a key trait of our Lord (Mark 5:19), and should be one of his followers as well (Philippians 2:1ff).

There is "kindness." This denotes a goodness of heart which causes us to act favorably toward all men. As a result of this kindness, we become as concerned for one another as we are for ourselves. As Paul exhorted the Ephesians to put on the wardrobe of the "new man," he referred to this article of clothing in these words, "*be ye kind to one another*" (4:32).

There is "humility." This is an attitude which places service to others and to God above service to self. We become anxious to see others served and their needs met. We are able to offer this service because of who we are— children of God and servants of the Almighty. This humility will cause us to share Paul's desire of personal sacrifice if it helps benefit the brethren (Philippians 2:17).

There is "meekness." This word is greatly misunderstood in our present day. It does not denote a cowardly shirking. It describes "strength under control." The meek person has the ability to keep all emotions under control. One has rendered this "gentleness," and perhaps that conveys the idea better. Once you have put on this article of clothing, you are able to deal gently with the trying ills of life and irritating people of life.

There is "longsuffering." Here is a piece of clothing that many of us have neglected to put on. Once we have put on this piece of clothing, we are able to suffer long with that trying person in life. Here is a patient endurance which foregoes malice and vindictiveness.

An ancient emperor of China was touring his realm and was entertained in a home that housed the master, his wife, children, daughter-in-law, grandchildren, and servants. All of these lived together in perfect harmony. The emperor was struck with admiration and asked the head of the house to inform him by what means quiet was kept among such a large number and variety of people. The old man took and pencil and wrote three words for the emperor to read—"Patience!"— "Patience!"— "Patience!"

If we want to find harmony and tolerance in the Lord's church, we need to put on this vital article of clothing. If you want help in developing this virtue, just consider the limitless patience of God in your life. If you can develop a patient longsuffering with others, as God has with you, you will find a great contentment!

There is "forbearing." Here is a willingness to suspend a rightful demand because of the weakness or immaturity of another. We are willing to follow our heavenly Father's example and be relenting, waiting for others to mature (cf. Romans 2:4; 3:25).

There is "forgiveness." This word is interesting to study. It comes from the same root as "grace." We are to demonstrate the same disposition to forgive one another as God possesses. Even when a gross injustice has been committed against us ["complaint"], we will have the desire to forgive.

Notice that Paul adds "as the Lord." The Lord forgives completely (Hebrews 8:12). He forgives readily when we admit wrong. We must learn to develop this willingness to forgive. Do not expect a person to "pay in blood" for some wrong committed against you. If asked, be willing to offer a full forgiveness. Be willing to treat the offending person better than you think he deserves because you are to forgive "as the Lord." We have received forgiveness from God; and in our forgiveness, we were treated far better than we deserved!

There may come times when we think that there is a good reason to retaliate, but as we "put on" Christ we have also put on this far-reaching forgiveness. Look at the following texts and see how crucial it is that we forgive one another just as God has forgiven us—Matthew 6:12, 14; 18:21-35; Luke 11:4; Mark 11:25.

There is "love." This love is the universal *AGAPE* which has the ability to love even the unloveable. "Above all" could be rendered "on the top of all." Using the clothing metaphor, we find that love is the final piece of clothing to be put on. It is to be like the "belt" or "girdle" which bound the loose flowing robes of the first century dress.

The only way that the other seven articles of clothing can be secured on the believer's person is by binding them with the girdle of love. Love completes the dress of the believer. Whenever love finds a home, then maturity will develop and will lead to a blessed unity. It is sad to see those who claim to follow the Supreme Savior, yet they have neglected to put on this vital article of clothing! *"Be ye therefore imitators of God, as beloved children; and walk in love, even as Christ also loved you, and gave himself up for us, an offering and a sacrifice to God for an odor of a sweet smell"* (Ephesians 5:1, 2).

Dear reader, remember this important piece of Christian clothing for you are never fully dressed without this girdle!

THE SAVIOR'S SUPREMACY WILL BECOME VISIBLE BY...
POSSESSING THE REALITY OF SALVATION (VS. 15, 16)

Whenever we have put on these items of clothing, we know beyond doubt that we possess the hope of heaven. We have been buried and have risen with Christ. We have put off and have put on!

Notice the following points which verify the assurance the believer possesses. The reality of salvation is verified by the presence of PEACE. This peace results from obeying God's will (Isaiah 57:20, 21). There is a "peace" which is offered by the world, but that kind of peace is never able to comfort and sustain as God's peace can (cf. John 14:27). This peace enables believers to live together in agreement.

From multiple backgrounds and cultures, the Lord's church provides a peaceful atmosphere for all to assemble together in a beautiful harmony and accord (cf. Colossians 3:10, 11). This peace will "rule" our lives. The Greek word used here refers to an umpire or arbitrator in games. As the believer struggles in the contests of life, the peace of the Savior enables the believer to find comfort. Those who fail to allow this peace to rule their lives will be like the "unstable man" in James 1:8. He will be tossed around with no fixed position or standard. The wonderful peace is said to be a "guard" in our thoughts and hearts (Philippians 4:7).

The reality of our salvation is verified by our ability to be THANKFUL (vs. 16b, 17). We are able to be thankful at all times and for all things because we know Christ is the Supreme Savior. Since we are His followers, there is nothing that can happen to us which will cause His supremacy to diminish. It is important to note that the inability to offer thanksgiving is a trait of one who is out of fellowship with God (cf. Romans 1:21).

The reality of our salvation is seen in DUTY. We are obligated to "teach" and to "admonish." This comes as a result of the Word of Christ dwelling in us. God's Word has become a permanent part of our lives and we cannot help but teach His truths. Our teaching is through "wisdom." We are careful to teach in a gentle and responsible way (2 Timothy 2:24-26).

It is interesting to observe that this teaching and admonishing can be carried out in a number of ways, but Paul specifically mentions the song service. Through the simple singing of psalms, hymns, and spiritual songs believers can teach, exhort, and admonish one another.

Unfortunately, the divinely designed mode of teaching has become distorted in modern times. Many see the song service as a period of entertainment and have added items to it which have taken it away from the divine purpose. There are those who fail to see the need for ALL members to participate in this method of praise and edification. They have reserved this mode of praise for a select "choir." Others have taken away the beauty of the first century acapella music and have added an instrument, or even entire bands!

Perhaps the best argument for remaining within the divine precepts and keeping our singing non-instrumental is offered in a comment heard on the news report which covered a large gathering of "Barber Shop Quartets." The question was asked to one group as to why they did not have an instrumental backup. The response was clear, "This kind of music was never designed for an instrumental accompaniment." Such is equally true with the song service in the worship assembly. It simply was never designed to be accompanied with instrumental music. Paul's lack of mention of any instrument is consistent with the plan of God for New Testament, and Old Testament, worship practices. Let each reader determine that he will participate in this divine pattern of worship!

DRAWING IT ALL TOGETHER

Is the Savior's supremacy as visible in your life as it was in the life of the pioneer at the beginning of this lesson? We have discovered three ways in which the Savior's Supremacy is to be visible—By your LIVING; by your CLOTHING; by your POSSESSION OF SALVATION.

There is an emphatic conclusion to this lesson on the Christian's dress stated by Christ in Matthew 22. It was customary for the wedding host to provide the wedding garments for the guests. The guests were expected to come clothed in the wedding garments given by the host. In Christ's parable, the invitation is sent out, the garments provided, and the wedding day comes. The invited guest arrived he is unclothed. "...*The king came in to behold the guests, he saw there a man who had not on a wedding-garment: and he saith unto him, 'Friend, how camest thou in hither not having a wedding-garment?"* And he was speechless. *Then the king said to the servants, 'Bind him hand and foot, and cast him out into the outer darkness; there shall be the weeping and the gnashing of teeth'"* (vs. 11-13). I am afraid that such could be the case with those in the Lord's church who have not "put on" the items of Christian clothing found in this passage.

Take a close careful look at the garment you have. Could it be that the words of James 5:2 apply to you? — *"Your riches are corrupted, and your garments are moth-eaten?"* Could it be that you have carefully put off and put on? The words of Revelation 3:4 reflect the urgency of wearing the proper clothing, "...*Thou has a few names in Sardis that did not defile their garments: and they shall walk with me in white; for they are worthy.*"

"*Blessed is he that watcheth, and keepeth his garments*" (Revelation 16:15b).

REFLECTION & RESOLUTIONS

Reflections from our study of Colossians 3:12-17:

1. Reflect upon the necessity of filling the spiritual void in our lives whenever we "put off" the old man of sin. Why is this a crucial action? Can you think of an illustration which shows the danger of failing either to put off ALL of the old man or failing to FILL the void completely?

2. Look closer at the word "elect." Find other passages where this is used. Does the Bible every speak about God's choosing individuals to either salvation or damnation? If God's election individual instead of a group? If so, what does this do for our hope of salvation?

3. Reflect on the reward of living the distinctive life. Do you think many members fully appreciate the great love of God? Find other passages which speak of God's great love for us.

4. Look closely at the "wardrobe" of the Christian. Is any one of these more important than the others? Why? Study each one and give a definition in your own words. Why do you think it is hardest for many to develop "longsuffering," 'forbearance," and "forgiveness?" What can we do to help us develop these?

Resolutions arising from our study of Colossians 3:12-17:

1. Resolve that, if you have not already done so, you will immediately "put off" and "put on."
2. Resolve that you will give a determined effort to developing the traits of the Christian's lifestyle found in this text.
3. Resolve that you will become fully clothed and never face the consequences found in Matthew 22:11-14.

[ii] Lipscomb, David. A Commentary on the New Testament Epistles (Ephesians, Philippians, and Colossians). The Gospel Advocate Commentary Series, Vol. IV. Gospel Advocate Company, Nashville, TN. 1968, p. 300.

═ 13 ═
THE LEAVEN OF CHRIST'S SUPREMACY

"Wives, be in subjection to your husbands, as is fitting in the Lord. Husbands, love your wives, and be not bitter against them. Children, obey your parents in all things, for this is well-pleasing in the Lord. Fathers, provoke not your children, that they be not discouraged. Servants, obey in all things them that are your masters according to the flesh; not with eye-service, as men-pleasers, but in singleness of heart, fearing the Lord; whatsoever you do, work heartily, as unto the Lord, and not unto men; knowing that from the Lord ye shall receive the recompense of the inheritance: ye serve the Lord Christ. For he that doeth wrong shall receive again for the wrong that he hath done: and there is no respect of persons. Masters render unto your servants that which is just and equal; knowing that ye also have a Master in heaven."
(Colossians 3:18–4:1)

Aristotle is reported as remarking that our society stands upon three great pairs of mutual relationships: "husband and wife, parent and child, master and slave." These are the three relationships which Paul brings our attention to focus on in the present passage. The great difference between Paul and Aristotle is not in the centuries separating their lives, but in the application of their teachings. Aristotle was concerned with the earthly while Paul was concerned with the spiritual. The one major difference separating Paul and Aristotle is the

Supreme Savior! These three relationships are crucial to our success, happiness, and joy in life. Each one of these can be quickly and permanently disrupted if we allow conflict to remain unresolved.

It is important to look closely at the context of this passage. In verse 17 Paul has just stated that the Savior's supremacy was to be demonstrated in "ALL" areas of living. Now Paul proceeds to give his readers specific illustrations of how the Lord's supremacy will change their lives. Here is perhaps the most practical application of Christ's supremacy found in this wonderful book.

As the passage is carefully read, it will be observed that the Savior's supremacy is like "leaven" in the believer's life. Leaven was a piece of bread dough which had fermented. It was dissolved into water and added to the next batch. It would slowly work until its effect was spread throughout the entire batch. Once leaven was introduced, its effect could not be stopped! In this passage, Paul teaches us that once the Savior's supremacy has been introduced into the lives of believers, its effect will not stop until every relationship has been changed. Ever so slowly, but surely, this "leaving" process will reach out and invade and transform the believer, making changes occur in these three crucial relationships. It is this "leavening" process and its results which Paul details in the present text.

THE LEAVENING OF YOUR MARRIAGE (3:18, 19)

Although the marriage institution is as old as man, Paul tells us that the leaven of the Savior will enable it to take on additional meaning. Using the points from the passage in Colossians as our basic structure, we examine the marriage union and observe how the leavening affects marriage.

First, Paul tells us that as the wife recognizes the Supreme Savior, there will be a leavening process which will change her (v. 18). Two points are seen from this verse: [1] The wife will be in subjection to her husband. 1 Peter 3:1-6 provides a further discussion on the concept of subjection and illustrates the point with a reference to Abraham and Sarah. [2] She will understand that she is following God's design for the marriage union by consenting to this subjection. This concept of subjection is scoffed at by many today who see it as a demeaning and humiliating servitude of women. Others have used the idea of subjection to assume, wrongly, that the husband has been given divine authority to exercise unlimited power over the wife. Some husbands have gone to the extreme in this belief to the extent that their wives cannot wear a certain color of clothing, or ribbon in her hair, or even get her hair cut! They conclude that the wife's subjection means that the man of the house is to make ALL decisions. It is sad to see the divine concept of subjection abused by either of these two extremes.

Because of the common abuse and misunderstanding regarding subjection, we need to examine it in great detail. From the Colossian text we are able to see that the subjection commanded by inspiration is best understood by looking at the three following points.

This subjection by the wife is prompted because of the man's love. The wife is willing to be in subjection to a husband who demonstrates the kind of love which verse 19 commands. This subjection is a voluntary response. It can never be forced upon the wife by a demanding husband.

I have personally known of marriages that eventually ended up "on the rocks" because the husband's pride was so warped that he forced his concept of subjection on his poor wife. Such a demanding attitude will eventually result in preposterous expectations from the husband for the wife. [One husband would call his wife every day five minutes before he left work and tell her to have his bath water drawn; and he expected it to be the "right" temperature. If the poor wife failed to do this, she never heard the end of it for a whole week!] Bible subjection of the wife to her husband is a voluntary response from the wife. If husbands want their wives to demonstrate this subjection, perhaps they had better begin to examine their actions and see if these actions encourage this voluntary subjection.

This subjection is "fitting in the Lord." Paul tells us that subjection in the marriage union is according to God's eternal design for the marriage (see 1 Corinthians 11:3). Any woman who desires to be in harmony with the plans of God will make sure that she is following God's design and is in subjection to her husband. Properly understood, the subjection of the wife is neither the husband's license for unreasonable and demanding order, nor is it relegating with wife to a position of servitude that is humiliating and demeaning.

Perhaps one verse that helps us to understand this concept best is found in Ephesians 5:21 where Paul says that the husband and the wife are to be in subjection to one another. Actually, this subjection is a two-way street. The marriage union is composed of two best friends who share the intimacies of marriage. They are concerned for one another and the will of God more than they are for self. The wife will look to her husband's counsel as a guiding friend's advice. She is willing to follow his decision, although this does not prevent her from communicating her own thoughts and desires before the final decision is made. This is a demonstration of the "love" that is taught to the younger women by the older women (Titus 2:4). There are a number of areas where this love and subjection can be demonstrated.

Let me suggest one area which seem to arise the most in sessions where problems are dividing the husband and wife—the appearance of the wife. I believe that many wives have been totally unaware of the great contrast that is often evident between their appearance and that of the women surrounding their husbands every day at work. Often this ignorance helps contribute to the failure of a marriage. Let me suggest a light-hearted look at this contrast and let each wife seriously consider her personal appearance as the husband arrives home. (Note: This illustration is from an earlier culture but it serves to illustrate the point.) At work the husbands are faced with women who take care and pride in the way their hair is set and styled. At home the husband is often greeted with a wife who is wearing last Sunday night's rollers, loosely hanging down. At work the husband is confronted with women who are neatly dressed; their clothes are clean, pressed, and pride is shown in the way they are worn. At home the husband arrives to find the wife still dressed in the dingy blue nightgown bought three years ago. At work the husband is greeted by women who are "fresh as a daisy." At home he is greeted by a "withered dandelion." At work the ladies are careful to speak with smiles; their words are pleasant, cheerful, and complimentary. At home, as soon as he arrives the husband is greeted with a list of everything that has gone wrong, reminded of the things he failed to do yesterday, and is pushed into the chore of immediately disciplining children who had been told "just wait until your father gets home!" At work the women are careful to put on some sweet-smelling perfume. At home the husband is greeted by a wife wearing the fragrance of "Lysol" or "Ajax." At work, the husband is around women who are concerned about the condition of their physical bodies; they take care to keep fit and muscles are in tone. At home the only thing athletic about their wife is that she wears the husband's old dingy-white tennis socks when her feet get cold.

Subjection is a broad and comprehensive command which all wives will quickly follow when they recognize the Savior's supremacy! Whenever the wife realizes Christ's supremacy, she will want to make her marriage relationship the very best possible. How sad it is to witness so many wives who do not care about the Lord's supremacy; they are devoted only to self. Such a selfish woman will never find the joy and fulfillment which God designed for the marriage union.

Second, Paul tells us that the husband will demonstrate the leavening of Christ's supremacy in his marriage (3:19). Two points are stressed by Paul. [1] Husbands will love their wives with *AGAPAO* love. [2] Husbands will never be bitter with their wives. It is crucial for men to understand what is meant by the command "love your wives." Our society has greatly confused the term "love." Paul leaves no doubt as to what "love" is meant to be. The use of the word *AGAPAO* identifies the husband's love as exactly that kind of love which God has shown the world. The key elements of this kind of love are sacrificing, serving, caring, and seeking the very best for the object loved. Men, this is a big order!

To the Ephesians Paul said that the husbands should love their wives just as they love their own bodies. This kind of love for the wife will see the husband doing things for the wife in an unselfish, serving manner, *"for no man ever hated his own flesh; but nourisheth and cherisheth it"* (Ephesians 5:29). Husbands, how do you show your wives that you really love them?

I recall trying to help a couple reconcile so that their marriage could be saved. The wife remarked, "After we get into a fight, all he thinks he has to do is to send me roses. I am sick of roses! Why doesn't he show me he is sorry instead of sending me those flowers?" That's a good question. Men, how often have you chosen "flowers" instead of sacrifice or service?

Husbands, when was the last time you showed your wife this *AGAPAO* love? This kind of love will control the authority which the man has in marriage. When you find a husband who truly demonstrates the love of verse 19, I guarantee that you will not find tyranny, cruelty, selfishness, and unkindness. Whenever the husband has developed this great love, he will be rewarded with a wife who is in subjection to his desires. A marriage is beautiful when it is guided by this deep and mutual love. This love does not just happen, it must be developed. This love of verse 19 is far superior to either physical or friendship love. It includes these, but it also goes far beyond these. When AGAPAO love exists in a marriage, it will build a foundation upon which the marriage union will last until death separates it.

A second point for the husbands to consider is found in the command not to be "bitter" with their wives. This command refers to the husband's disposition and attitudes. Husbands have no right in harboring resentment, or showing a harsh and unfeeling disposition. Husbands would do well to compare their attitudes with those of Nabal in 1 Samuel 25. Here is a husband acting opposite to the command in Colossians

3:19. In fact, it is safe to say that not only did Nabal fail to show this love, but he was also "bitter" with Abigail. Nabal is described as a husband who was "churlish" (harsh) and evil in his dealings. Because of this man's attitudes, the Bible states that folly was with him. The punishment of God was quick in coming (1 Samuel 25:38).

Husbands, you had better make sure that your attitudes stand in dramatic contrast to those of Nabal! Husbands must not be irritable or surly with their wives. If they persist in this type of attitude and conduct, they will be living contrary to the will of God. Such men have not allowed the supremacy of the Savior to "rule" their words and deeds. It is heartbreaking to see some good sisters in the Church struggle with husbands who are bitter. Nothing they ever do is right; there is never a kind word of appreciation spoken; everything is always wrong. I like the remark that someone has made in connection with this point, "It is useless to call your wife 'honey' if you act like vinegar toward her."

Husbands, how do you measure up with these two points? Have you allowed the Savior's supremacy to renovate you so that your wife is able to see the difference? Do you show the kind of love toward her that enables her to know that she is the one special person in your life? Have you verbally told her recently how much you love her and how glad you are that you married her?

It is a great tragedy that in our nation the divorce rate has skyrocketed. Those who enter into marriage form a covenant with one another, and with God, which should never be broken. Yet, it is a sobering reality that many marriages fail. The divorce decree may read one of the many causes for the marriage's failure, but there is one reason explaining the failure. Either one or both of the marriage partners failed to recognize and follow the

Savior's supremacy. Let the Savior's supremacy leaven your marriage relationship!

THE LEAVENING OF YOUR HOME (3:20, 21)

As the greatest crisis of our modern society is the home. There is an ever-increasing demand for family counselors who have developed the talent to sit down with parents and children and assist them to resolve the conflicts which threaten to destroy their relationship. In these two verses, the Apostle brings a focused application on how the Savior's supremacy will leaven the Christian family and enable it to become the warm and beautiful unit that God designed it to be.

First, Paul addresses the children (3:20). "Children" refers to those young people who have reached the age where they choose to obey or disobey. The tiny tot is trained in right and wrong by the parents. This tot does right because of constant training; he has not yet reached that age where he will reason and then act. As the child matures, he reaches the age where his behavior is decided by his choice—not his parents'. The child will choose to obey or disobey. It is to the children who have grown to the stage of choosing for themselves that the Apostle's words are addressed.

Those who are old enough to make personal decisions must be influenced by the supremacy of the Savior. There is only one thing that the child, who recognizes Christ's supremacy, is going to do— "obey!" The word "obey" comes from a word which means "to listen at the door." The image presented by this word is that of a child who hears a knock at the door and quickly goes to answer it. As the door is opened, the child is given instructions and closely pays attention. When the instructions have ended, the child runs to carry out the message. Children are thus commanded to listen carefully to their parents' counsel and then quickly carry out that counsel. The obedience is to be in "all things."

The child should obey the parents in all things because he is the child and mom and dad are the parents. It is easy for children to obey their parents in the easy and agreeable chores. But the child who realizes that Jesus Christ is the Supreme Savior is going to make sure that he or she obeys parents in "all" things—whether they think these things are "fair" or not. The reason for this complete obedience is stated, it *pleases* God. This kind of obedience is beautiful. It brings happiness and harmony to the home. *"My son, keep thy father's commandment, and forsake not the law of thy mother"* (Proverbs 6:20). Paul is talking directly to the young people. Because they are old enough to make responsible choices, they must obey. Disobedience to parents has always carried disastrous consequences. *"He who curses his father or mother shall surely be put to death" (Exodus 21:17, NASV).* *"Every one of you shall reverence his mother and father...If there is anyone who curses his father or his mother...his bloodguiltiness is upon him"* (Leviticus 19:3; 20:9, NASV).

Let the children seriously consider these points—Are you behaving properly toward your parents? Do you show them the proper respect? Are you "obeying" them in "all" things? Do you see the disastrous consequences which await you if you are not allowing the Savior's supremacy to leaven your relationship with your parents?

Second, Paul addresses the parents (3:21). "Fathers" is better understood when we translate it as "parents" (Hebrews 11:23). Paul is not speaking only to the fathers, but also to the mothers. Hence, the command is to the "parents."

Paul looks at how the parents discipline children and he says for parents to be careful of two extremes—do not be overbearing and do not be too lenient. Parents should not expect the child to obey some absurdity. Parents should expect the child to respect and honor their position. Parents should be reasonable in expecting children to obey their wishes. After all, they are the parents and the children are the children. Parents should allow their children to act as children, but as well-disciplined children.

The word "provoke" describes the reaction of the child when parents use unjust discipline. Literally the word means "to irritate." The parent should be careful not to cause the child to feel "irritated." Now, some parents refuse to expect their children to do anything; the child is free to do as he pleases because the parents do not want to 'irritate" them. Such a notion is completely opposite of what Paul teaches here.

Parents need to train the child, but they must be careful that the rules are not harsh or inconsistent. Inconsistent discipline is disastrous to the child. It causes the child to feel frustrated and anxious about what pleases the parent. In talking with some teens about this point, it was expressed that some parents are always changing what they expect from the child. One young man expressed this frustration to me as he related his efforts at trying to please parents. When his parent expressed dissatisfaction with something he did, he tried to change. But even with change, he was still met with a disapproving remark. As a consequence, he was totally frustrated, or as Paul says "provoked." This word communicates a constant fault-finding and criticism. The parent never bolsters the child's self-image and self-worth. It is good for the parent to stop and ask, "When was the last time I told ___ how much I appreciate his/her willingness and cooperation?"

It is easy for parents to say "No!" without stopping to listen to what their child is asking. Far too many parents automatically say "No" to the child when the child wants to do some little harmless thing. Parents, we need to be careful how we use "No" in talking with our children. After considering the point, it is easy to understand why some children never take their parents seriously when they are told "No." They hear it all the time!

I recall being at the Blue Ridge Family Bible Encampment in 1983 and listening to the speaker at the Fireside Chats. He was relating how his little granddaughter had been taught to imitate the sounds of various animals. He would ask her to tell him how the cow, horse, turkey, etc. sounded. After the list of animals had been exhausted, he asked, "Now, tell me how mommy sounds?" The little girl said, "Mommy says 'No, No, No!'" Parents, if your child was asked, "How does mommy (or daddy) sound?" what would the answer be? Notice that Paul says when parents use inconsistent, unreasonable, or harsh discipline, the child will be "provoked" and become "discouraged." They "lose heart" and become sullen and listless.

I remember talking with a parent who came to my office saying that his child had stopped talking with him and his wife. After several periods with both parents and the son, it was discovered that the problem rested in the point we are studying—the inconsistent parents had frustrated the child. The child saw no way to please the parents, so he simply stopped talking. Brother David Lipscomb makes an excellent comment on this point.

He who always finds fault with a child, who is never satisfied with what he does, who scolds, and frets, and complains, let him do what he will, breaks the spirit, and even destroys all desire of doing well. The child, in despair, soon gives up every effort to please." [iii]

What practical points Paul gives! When parents and children recognize the supreme position of Christ, they are going to develop the best relationship with one another that is possible. Let me suggest the following points to both parents and children, which if used, will help the Savior's supremacy develop this beautiful relationship.

(1) Each parent and child should realize that the other is human. As such, there will be failings and shortcomings. Parent are not perfect and they will make some bad decisions. They are not always right. But the children are less mature and do not have the maturity of their parents. Children are in no position to usurp the divine structure of the family. Parents need to realize that children are not perfect when they are born into this world. They need training. Some need more training than others. Parents must offer patient discipline which encourages their child to mature in a balanced manner.

(2) Parents need to make time to listen to their children. Far too many parents are very selfish with their time. Many children want to talk with their parents, but the parents never make time to be available—it is always the job, the hobby, the adult friends, and seldom the child! This point was brought home to me one afternoon. I had just arrived home from work and was worn out. All I wanted was to spend some time in quiet isolation, away from all the distractions of life. I thought I had found the

perfect refuge when my six-year-old son came into the room. He had been busy at school and there was something important he had to tell me. As he entered the room, I look at him and gruffly asked, "What are YOU doing in here?" He stopped, and with a hurt look, softly responded, "Dad! I just wanted to talk with you!" Needless to say, those simple words burned deeply and as a result I always try to put aside whatever I am doing and listen carefully when my child needs to "just talk" with me. What about you? Do you put aside "things" so that you and your children can "just talk?"

(3) Parents should verbally encourage children and children verbally encourage parents. When was the last time that you told one another how much you love each other? When was the last time you told one another how much you appreciate the kind things done for you? Do not assume that the other knows how you feel. Make sure they know!

(4) Parents need to make sure their discipline is proper, but no absurd.

(5) Children ought to respect and conform to the parents' rules and decisions. In one of Ann Lander's articles (an advice column that used to appear in newspapers), a young lady wrote:

> *"Dear Ann: This is for 'Embattled.' I was 18 once and, just like those headstrong, selfish daughters, I thought I should be allowed to do whatever I wanted. After some major hassles, my parents said, 'OK, you're an adult now. Do as you please.' I did. At the end of the month my father presented me with a bill for rent, food, my share of the utilities and telephone, along with a 'service charge' for laundry, dry cleaning, and*

housekeeping. When I added everything up, my attitude changed in a hurry. Sign me Chastened" [The St. Louis Post Dispatch, June 1, 1983].

Once children sit down and look at all their parents do for them, they should see their duty to obey in a respectful way.

THE LEAVENING OF YOUR DAILY JOB (3:22-4:1)

The leaven of the Savior does not stop at your home. It goes far beyond that domicile. In this section Paul shows us that the Savior's influence will be seen in our daily jobs. Whether you are management or labor you are going to be affected.

To the employees Paul says your attitude and actions in work will be changed (3:22-25). There are other references in the New Testament to this work ethic of the Christian (1 Thessalonians 4:11, 12; 2 Thessalonians 3:10, 11; Ephesians 6:5-9; 1 Timothy 6:1, 2; Titus 2:9, 10; 1 Peter 2:18-23). Space does not allow a thorough discussion of each of these texts, but it is evident that the Christian employee is drastically different from others.

Christ's supremacy has instilled in the Christian employee obedience to superiors, responsibility in working, and personal integrity in business affairs. The employee who serves the Supreme Savior is challenged to rise above the ordinary. In fact, the Christian employee's motto was "Quality is Job 1" long before Ford Motor Company had it! The Christian employee is looking forward to the welcome of Matthew 25:21, *"...Well done, good and faithful servant: thou hast been faithful over a few things, I will set thee over many things; enter thou into the joy of thy Lord."* The fact that our behavior on the daily job will affect our eternal destiny is clear from verses 24-

25. Let every employee make sure that the Savior's supremacy governs his work habits.

To the employers Paul says that your lives will also experience the leavening of the Savior (3:25; 4:1). There will be diligence to make sure that you are fair and equal toward all of your workers. You will be a responsible manager of those who labor under you. You will recognize the need to be fair and equal because that is how you want the Savior to treat you— "you also have a Master in heaven." One of the greatest joys possible is to work under an employer, or supervisor, who is a faithful Christian. The employer will also be judged according to the principles of 3:24, 25.

DRAWING IT ALL TOGETHER

What a practical section of scripture! The Savior's supremacy will act as leaven and influence the way we act in the three important relationships of life. If the Savior's supremacy has not yet leavened your conduct in these three relationships, look carefully at 3:25 because those words apply to you.

Let's close this lesson with a personal exam. Ask yourself these questions and honestly answer each one.

Wives—are you performing your role acceptably? Do you render proper subjection? Do you make sure that you are doing everything you can to make your home a happy and peaceful place for your husband to come home to each day?

Husbands—Are you loving your wives with that *AGAPAO* love? Do you sacrifice, serve, and care for your wife? How does she see your attitude? Is it "bitter?" Are you content to give "roses" instead of sacrifice and service?

Children—Are you obeying your parents? Do you love and honor them? Do you show them respect?

Parents—Do you provoke and discourage? Are you disciplining your children in a responsible, godly way?

Employees—Are you laboring "unto the Lord?" Are you honest, dependable, energetic, and respectful?

Employers—Are you fair and equal? Do you supervise others as you wish your "Master in heaven" to supervise you?

Remember—You can never be a success in any of these crucial relationships of life until you allow the Savior's supremacy to touch every relationship.

REFLECTIONS & RESOLUTIONS

Reflections from our study of Colossians 3:18-4:1:

1. Reflect on each of the three relationships discussed in this section. Is any one of these more important than the others? Why? Why do you think Paul included the employee/employer relationship with the other two? Why would he use the terms "masters" and "slaves?"

2. Reflect on the husband/wife relationship. Add three other ways to the list of how a wife can show subjection to her husband. Do you think the idea of subjection is a "put-down" on women? How can the husband show his love to his wife? Do you think many husbands take this point for granted? Why? Discuss further how the husband can be "bitter."

3. Reflect on the parent/child relationship. Find other references in the Bible which show how this relationship should be governed. List three points which you think are crucial to the relationship. What things will cause this relationship to be destroyed? If

a parent/child relationship is destroyed, what can be done to help it be restored? List three good books which use Scriptural principles to strengthen the parent/child relationship.

4. Reflect on the employee/employer relationship. Look up the other references to this relationship and make a list of guiding principles for the Christian worker. From this list, select four which you feel are the most important.

Resolutions arising from our study of Colossians 3:18-4:1:

1. Resolve that you will do everything you can to strengthen your marriage.

2. Resolve that as either a parent or child, you will make sure your home is a wonderful place in which the Savior's supremacy rules.

3. Resolve that as a Christian worker your work habits and attitudes reflect the Savior's supremacy.

[iii] Lipscomb, David. A Commentary on the New Testament Epistles (Ephesians, Philippians, and Colossians). The Gospel Advocate Commentary Series, Vol. IV. Gospel Advocate Company, Nashville, TN. 1968, p. 304.

═ 14 ═
HANKERINGS FOSTERED BY THE SUPREME SAVIOR

"Continue steadfastly in prayer, watching therein with thanksgiving; withal praying for us also, that God may open unto us a door for the word, to speak the mystery of Christ, for which I am also in bonds; that I may make it manifest as I ought to speak. Walk in wisdom toward them that are without, redeeming the time. Let your speech be always with grace, seasoned with salt. Let your speech be always with grace, seasoned with salt, that ye may know how ye ought to answer each one."
(Colossians 4:2-6)

A young man wanted to be a missionary; but his worldly and wealthy father thought he was too good for that. So, he made a merchant of him. The young man went sadly about his daily task. Like the statue of Columbus at Genoa which is made to every look longingly westward, the heart of the disappointed young man would look longingly toward the ministry—toward the sublime services of the Lord Jesus Christ. These longings held the attention and vision of the young man. All that he wanted and desired was this deep "hankering" for service.

Within this passage we are able to discover some strong desires that were ever present in the Apostle's mind. As the young man kept constant thought on the mission field, so Paul constantly thought on the points of our present lesson.

As the passage is viewed overall, it will be observed that Paul closes the practical exhortation of the book with emphasis upon development in two areas of life—the spiritual and the physical. Paul exhorts the Colossians to develop their spirituality by a greater devotion and trust in God. In the physical area, Paul urges believers to keep a close watch on how they react to the non-believer. Once again, we are able to mark three prominent aspects of Christianity that are often stressed by Paul—steadfast praying, responsible stewardship, and devoted example.

Look at the passage and carefully consider these deep longings which the Apostle shared for believers. These "hankerings" were developed because of the conviction which Paul possessed about the Savior's supremacy. It did not matter where Paul was, he thought about these things. Even while under lock and chain, these weighed heavily upon his mind.

PAUL STRONGLY DESIRED...
THAT OTHERS WOULD KNOW THE JOY OF PRAYER (4:2, 3A)

Whenever I think of the great Apostle Paul, one of the most common images I see is that of a man in deep, earnest prayer! Paul saw prayer as a great blessing. He realized that only through prayer would the believer be able to withstand the fiery darts of the Tempter and would be in a position to receive the warm welcome of the Judge on the last day. In every epistle which Paul writes, you will find a number of references to the duty, privilege, necessity, and blessing of prayer.

As Paul listed the various pieces of the Christian's armor in Ephesians 6, there is an interesting piece omitted. An important piece of protection to the Roman soldiers were the "graves," a protection for the shins and knees. It is interesting to see the failure of Paul to list these. But, let me suggest that this was a deliberate omission. Paul was well aware that the greatest protection for the Christian's knees was prayer! When the Christian is set in humble prayer, there can be no greater defense and protection. Thus, Ephesians 6:18 stresses the need for believing prayer, *"With all prayer and supplication praying at all seasons in the Spirit, and watching thereunto in all perseverance and supplication for all the saints."*

From these verses we are able to discover some basic principles which will allow us to know the joy of praying:

First, there must be DEVOTION— *"continue steadfastly."* Here we find that a certain persistence and determination must be evident in our prayer habits. We must resolve that we will not grow weary or give up. Our Lord stressed this determined devotion when He commanded that we "ought always to pray, and not to faint" (Luke 18:1). When Paul encourages us to *"continue steadfastly,"* he is urging that we develop a strong and stubborn pattern in our prayers. Once we do this, we will never become slack in appointing regular times of prayer with God.

It is so easy to be deflected from our duty of devoted prayer. Sometimes we allow ourselves to be caught up in activities that take all of our time and energy, and we just do not have time for praying. It is said of some Japanese that instead of spending their time in listening to a sermon, the march decorously to the temple where their priests are performing services. They arrive at the temple and throw in a printed prayer with a little money and then hurriedly go about their business with a satisfied conscience. One has to wonder if we are not often guilty of a similar thing. How often do we hurriedly utter some prayer, with little thought, time-worn phrases, and then go about our business with a soothed conscience?

To *"continue steadfastly"* in prayers means we will be stubborn enough not to allow our prayers to be misplaced or misdirected. This steadfastness was very visible in the lives of our first century brethren. *"These all with one accord continued steadfastly in prayer"* (Acts 1:14).

Ask yourself, "Do I demonstrate this steadfastness in my personal prayers?" A little boy said his prayers as he prepared to go to bed. As he prayed, his prayerless father stood by listening. The child rose from his knees and as he jumped into bed asked, "Now, daddy, I have said my prayers, have you said yours?" The father replied that he had not. With the innocence of youth, the tiny tot asked, "Daddy, are you too big to pray?" One often wonders if many adult believers, who have forgotten the joys of praying, think they are "too big to pray."

Second, there must be ALERTNESS— *"watching."* This word suggests a constant awareness in prayers. You are "on guard." You are concentrating your thoughts upon the words you are speaking. As we "watch" in prayer, we will be careful to do the following: [1] We will be careful that our minds do not become distracted. It is easy to be praying about a pressing need and, as that need is mentioned, you allow your mind to dwell upon it until you are caught up with it instead of your heavenly Father. [2] We will concentrate our thoughts in an earnest effort and become like the godly Epaphras who is forever remembered as "striving" for others in his prayers. [3] We will be keenly aware of our personal needs, the present dangers around us, and the great and good promises of God.

As the Lord took Peter, James, and John into the deeper recesses of Gethsemane, He urged them, "*Watch and pray, that ye enter not into temptation: the spirit indeed is willing, but the flesh is weak*" (Mark 14:38). Such an admonition is fitting for modern believers as they pray.

Third, there should be GRATITUDE— "*thanksgiving.*" This is the sixth time Paul has mentioned the virtue to our Colossian brethren. Paul wanted believers to be thankful in their prayers. This is an oft neglected element in many prayers. It seems that many times we are more concerned about expressing our wants than in offering words of appreciation for what God has already done for us. Thanksgiving is essential to joy-filled prayers because it enables us to recall past blessings which we have received from God. If God has answered past prayers, we can rest assured that He will continue to do so.

With gratitude being shown in our prayers, we can approach God in a confident manner and lay before Him our pressing needs. Thanksgiving will move us to spontaneous praise. Whenever fortunate benefits are received, we will pause to offer appreciation to God for what has just happened to us. Thanksgiving will enable us to be strong in the face of adversity, "*In nothing be anxious; but in everything by prayer and supplication with thanksgiving, let your requests be made known unto God*" (Philippians 4:6).

Fourth, there will be HUMILITY— "*for us also.*" Humility is necessary if we ask others to pray for us. Humility should be evident in our attitude as we approach God's merciful throne in prayer. It is amazing to me to see some people approach God in prayer as if they are doing God a big favor by praying to Him. Humility should be seen as we seek good for other in our prayers, and as we ask Him for our personal needs.

Paul had a deep "hankering" for the Colossians to know the joy of believing prayer. Why does the Savior's supremacy make praying such a joy-filled labor? Because as the Supreme Savior He is in control of everything and, thus, has the power to answer all of our needs. Also, as our Supreme Savior, we have access to Him so that He will listen and guarantee an answer. "And w*hatsoever we ask we receive of him, because we keep his commandments and do the things that are pleasing in his sight*" (1 John 3:22).

PAUL STRONGLY DESIRED...
OPPORTUNITIES TO TEACH THE GOSPEL (4:3B, 4)

Even in prison and constantly chained to the Roman soldier, Paul's desire to spread the Word of Christ is prominent. This is a most amazing point to consider. He has been tried and was waiting for Nero's verdict. Had we been in his place, I am sure we would have fretted about the outcome—but not Paul! Paul's eagerness is a logical reflection of his intense devotion to the Lord. In fact, he had told the Corinthians that his intense eagerness to preach and teach Christ was due to the fact that the love of Christ "constrained" him (cf. 2 Corinthians 5:14). It did not matter to Paul if he were in prison or the free marketplace; he was going to seek opportunities to preach and teach the gospel (Ephesians 6:19).

Look closer at this point. Paul was saying, "I want to work! I want to find an open door of opportunity!" He understood that opportunity was an "open door" which could be closed. It must be seized before it was shut (cf. 1 Corinthians 16:9; 2 Corinthians 2:12). To Paul every person was, if not a potential convert, at least an audience to listen to the grand gospel message. Paul's desire had a noble objective—to make the message so clear than anyone who listened would understand (v. 4). He wanted to seize every chance and speak clearly and simply.

This desire is desperately needed in the Lord's church today. How often do you seek opportunities to teach and preach the gospel of Christ? What is your level of contentment for using opportunities in the Lord's service? Are you content to do as little as possible? Are you like Paul, always seeking to do "your share" and then some? Do you realize that opportunity must be grasped while the door is still "open?" I like the old Latin proverb that speaks of our need to use opportunities quickly, "opportunity has hair in front; behind she is bald: if you seize her by the forelock, you may hold her; but if suffered to escape, not even Jupiter himself can catch her again."

As the four starving lepers walked into the Syrian camp, they discovered the camp deserted and food in abundance. Then they thought, "*We are not doing right. This day is a day of good news, but we are keeping silent; if we wait until morning light, punishment will overtake us. Now therefore come, let us go and tell...*" (2 Kings 7:9, NASV). Their message saved the starving city only because they did not hesitate.

Let us learn from them and realize that we possess the greatest message possible; but it is worthless to those around us unless we seize opportunities as Paul did. Often, we allow hardship and trial to cause our opportunities to be missed. Paul asks that we join him and "suffer hardships" so that the Cause of Christ will spread (2 Timothy 2:3). Do you share this strong "hankering" of Paul?

PAUL STRONGLY DESIRED...
THAT BELIEVERS LIVE AN EXEMPLARY LIFE (4:5-6)

This exemplary life must be guided by wisdom (v. 5a). The believer's objective should be like Paul's, "*that the life also of Jesus may be manifested in our mortal flesh*" (2 Corinthians 4:11b). This wisdom will make sure that our lives are discreet and commendable. I think that one of the finest comments on this point has been made by David Lipscomb:

> ... those claiming to be Christians. It has always been so, and is true today. They watch our walk more than our talk, and judge and measure our talk by our walk. To benefit other spiritually, the chief qualification is not gifts, but character. The lives of Christians are the Bible the world reads. (2 Corinthians 3: 2, 3). We should see that the text is not corrupted or illegible. Live so that the more you are known the more you will be esteemed, so that those who are without and anxious would naturally seek you for help and guidance, and your judgment or reproof would carry with it the weight of a consecrated character." [iv]

This exemplary life uses every opportunity (v. 5b). Paul wants every believer to be just as determined to spread the gospel as he is. How far would the gospel spread if every Christ were as concerned and active as you presently are? The image presented by Paul in the expression "redeem the time" is that of a shopper who comes upon a bargain. The bargain is immediately seized or it will be lost. Literally, Paul commands us to "buy up opportunity." Every moment of life is a unique and precious gift that must be jealously guarded. We all have the same 24 hours in a day, yet some are able to accomplish far more than others. Why? Simply because they are wiser in using their time. The believer's life will be one that seizes every opportunity to serve God. He/she does not just sit back and wait!

This exemplary life uses "seasoned speech (v. 6). Notice that Paul says this kind of speech is to be used "always." Care is taken about how we speak; not because of who we are around, but because of who we have become! We are always careful to speak properly—under all circumstances and around all people. Paul gives us a list of the spices which season the speech of the exemplary life.

First, there is GRACE. Grace causes our speech to be graceful, gentle, beautiful, attractive, pleasant, and kind. It was this quality which caused the Lord's speech to be noticed. *"And all bare him witness, and wondered at the words of grace which proceeded out of his mouth..."* (Luke 4:22).

Second, there is SALT. Whenever we think of "salty speech" we generally think of cursing and foul language. However, such is not the "salty speech" that characterizes the exemplary life. This is the kind of "salt" that Christ refers to in Matthew 5:13. When we use this salty speech of the exemplary life, our words will be able to accomplish the following: there will be preservation from corruption; a purified and wholesome atmosphere will be encouraged; life will be flavored for the better; and, an appetite for God's Word will be cultivated.

Third, there is SENSITIVITY. We learn to adapt our speech to the hearer so that we will not offend. Our speech will be appropriate to the person we are addressing. The duty we share to speak in a sensitive manner is shown by two phrases in the text, "*that I may make it manifest, as I ought to speak*" (v. 4), and "*...that ye may know how ye ought to answer each one*" (v. 6b). There have been countless injuries inflected on others because someone failed to demonstrate this sensitivity in speech of the exemplary life. We need to pray with the Psalmist, "*Set a guard, O Lord, over my mouth: Keep watch over the door of my lips*" (Psalm 141:3, NASV). Let us make sure we have our speech seasoned with the spice of sensitivity.

DRAWING IT ALL TOGETHER

Paul was a wonderful man who shared deep desires for his fellow brethren. He thought of these desires whenever he considered the spiritual condition of his brethren. His desires can best be grouped into three major thoughts: He wanted them to know the great joy of praying; He wanted them to know of his great desire to find opportunities to preach the gospel of Christ; He wanted them to know of his strong desire that believers live an exemplary lifestyle.

Do you share these "hankerings" as Paul? When you think of your brethren, do your thoughts center on desires for their maturity and the gospel's advancement? May each reader realize that when he follows the Supreme Savior, these "hankerings" will be fostered by that realization?

REFLECTIONS & RESOLUTIONS

Reflections from our study of Colossians 4:2-6:

1. Reflect on the great joy which results from a daily practice of believing prayer. Do you think most believers enjoy this great blessing? Why? What do

you suggest Christians do to realize the great blessing and joy in believing prayer?

2. Reflect on the basic principles of prayer discovered in this text. Which is the most important to you? Why? Arrange them in order of importance.

3. Reflect on the need to seize opportunities in life. Why must opportunity be seized "quickly?" How is it possible for one to "buy up opportunity?" Look through the Bible and list some occasions where opportunity was allowed to slip past. List some opportunities that you have allowed to slip past, then some which you have seized?

4. Reflect on the importance of an exemplary life. Why is one's speech so important to living the proper example? How does the word "always" qualify the speech of believers? Look at the "wisdom" which directs the exemplary life. Find other texts which speak of this wisdom.

Resolutions arriving from our study of Colossians 4:2-6:

1. Resolve that you will begin to develop the kind of stubborn and steadfast prayer life that believers should possess.

2. Resolve that you will follow Paul's example and seek out opportunities to spread the gospel message.

3. Resolve that you will change in every area so that your life will be "exemplary" and fitting for the Lord's service.

[iv] Lipscomb, David. A Commentary on the New Testament Epistles (Ephesians, Philippians, and Colossians). The Gospel Advocate

Commentary Series, Vol. IV. Gospel Advocate Company, Nashville, TN. 1968, p. 308.

= 15 =
A CHORUS SINGS CHRIST'S SUPREMACY

"All my affairs shall Tychicus make known unto you, the beloved brother and faithful minister and fellow-servant in the Lord: whom I have sent unto you for this very purpose, that ye may know our state, and that he may comfort your hearts; together with Onesimus, the faithful and beloved brother, who is one of you. They shall make known unto you all things that are done here. Aristarchus my fellow-prisoner saluteth you, and Mark, the cousin of Barnabas (touching whom ye received commandments; if he come unto you, receive him), and Jesus that is called Justus, who are of the circumcision: these only are my fellow-workers unto the kingdom of God, men that have been a comfort unto me. Epaphras, who is one of you, a servant of Christ Jesus, saluteth you, always striving for you in his prayers, that ye may stand perfect and fully assured in all the will of God. For I bear him witness, that he hath much labor for you, and for them in Laodicea, and for them in Hierapolis. Luke, the beloved physician, and Demas salute you. Salute the brethren that are in Loaodicea, and Nymphas, and the church that is in their house. And when this epistle hath been read among you, cause that it be read also in the church of the Laodiceans; and that ye also read the epistle from Laodicea. And say to Archippus, 'Take heed to the ministry which thou hast received in the Lord, that thou fulfill it.' The salutation of me Paul with mine own hand. Remember my bonds. Grace be with you."
(Colossians 4:7-18)

In 1869 the city of Boston was the place of the great "Peace Jubilee," which was sung in celebration of the ending of the Civil War. There was a chorus of 10,000 voices and an orchestra of 1,000 pieces. Two hundred anvils had been placed on the platform for use in the "anvil chorus." There were huge bells; and outside the park was artillery to be fired by electricity in harmony with the chorus. At the head of the two hundred violins stood the world's greatest violinist, Ole Bull, who had them so trained that their bows worked as if in the hand of a single man. Parepa-Rosa was the soloist, of whose singing that day one remarked, "It will never be equaled again on earth." When in the "Star Spangled Banner" she sang the high "C" with the accompaniment of the full chorus and orchestra, the bells and the cannon, it was so loud and so clear that it could be heard for miles around. The acclaim of the choral performance spread to all parts of the country.

As magnificent as the great chorus of Boston's "Peace Jubilee" was, we open our Bibles to a greater chorus. From a small group of believers listed in these closing verses, we are able to hear a song service that remains unmatched—except among faithful brethren who continue to serve the Supreme Savior.

It is often tempting to pass over the long lists of odd and unfamiliar names that are normally found in the conclusion of the epistles. We often do not even venture an attempt at pronouncing many of these names. But, if we skip over these lists, we will fail to discover some very important lessons. Let me suggest that in this list of odd and unfamiliar names at the close of the Colossian epistle, we have a "chorus." This chorus sings in harmony about the Savior's supremacy. As we closely look at this section, we will discover a most fitting conclusion to a book that has spoken so clearly about the Savior's supremacy. Carefully consider the verses and observe the following parts of this choral group:

IN THIS GROUP WE DISCOVER...
TWO DUETS WHICH SING OF THE SUPREMACY OF CHRIST'S CHURCH

The first duet is composed of Tychicus and Onesimus (vs. 7-9). Tychicus is referred to in other New Testament texts (cf. Ephesians 6:21; Acts 20:4; 2 Timothy 4:12; Titus 3:12). From the other passages describing the first century brother, we are able to see that he was often used by Paul as a messenger. He delivered the Ephesian epistle; he was sent to Crete to relieve Titus; later he was sent to Ephesus to allow Timothy any opportunity to visit Paul in his final days.

It appears that Tychicus was one of those who traveled to Jerusalem as a representative of the Gentile Christians offering benevolent alms to his Jewish brethren. When you read the various texts about Tychicus, there seems to be one prominent fact—no matter what the chore was, he was willing to do it! One author noted that in Paul's use of the word "faithful" he stressed the dependability of Tychicus. Here was a brother who would accept a job and see that it was carried out in the proper way.

The second member of this duet is Onesimus. Here is a most interesting person. He was a thief and a runaway slave. He had taken advantage of his master. In running to the Imperial City, Onesimus had hoped to become lost in the great multitudes and escape capture. But in the providential workings of God, this slave had arrived in the city only to be converted by the gospel of Jesus Christ. After his conversion, he had become a loved and accepted member of the congregation.

Soon he realized that the Supreme Savior demands full devotion and that meant he had to make restitution of his errors. He determined to do whatever was within his power to correct his past wrongs. He set about to return to his former master. Once again, we are able to catch sight of the great providential working of God in this man's life. Onesimus' master was Philemon, one of the stalwart members of the Colossian church. Onesimus was to return home armed with the short epistle to Philemon in which Paul asks the master to receive his runaway slave back as a brother in the Lord. From this duet we are able to see how great the Savior's church is.

First, they teach us that our past is not present. It does not matter how wicked we once were. We could have been a thief and a runaway slave, but the Savior's supremacy erases the past. This message of peace and pardon needs to be realized by many members in the Lord's body today. If the Savior is supreme in your life, then His supremacy has erased your past!

Second, this duet teaches that in the church we are able to find a wonderful fellowship bond. Look carefully at the passage and notice how these two brethren emphasize fellowship. Fellowship "comforts" (v. 7). Literally, this word means to "encourage" another to stand firm against error and remain pure. When you share in the blessed fellowship bond of the Lord's church, you will be encouraged to remain faithful and pure. From the phrase, "know our state," we find that this fellowship bond allows us to be honest and open with one another. Paul was anxious that the brethren in Colossae, whom he had never met, know all about his circumstances and needs. Such honesty is a wonderful blessing in the church. Fellowship with one another should allow us to feel comfortable in asking for help and prayers. The word "together" (v. 9) is a good summary of this fellowship bond. Here would be two brethren coming "together" to deliver a message from a beloved apostle to a group of others who share a like faith. This togetherness should be a marked trait of the Lord's people because we share in a blessed fellowship.

A *third* lesson which these two men teach centers on the truth that in the Lord's church we are privileged to share relationships with one another that are not possible elsewhere. Look carefully at how Paul refers to Tychicus. He is a "beloved brother," a "faithful minister," and a "fellow servant." You cannot share in these relationships unless you are in subjection to the Savior's supremacy. To be a "brother" means that you have come from the "same source, the same origin." This unique origin is possible only as we rest in God's family as His children. To be a "minister' means that you are willing to be a helper or assistant. However, the directions and attitudes of this minister are vague unless you are certain of divine inspiration. To be a "servant" means that you are a "bond-servant." This refers to one who has subjected himself to an absolute devotion and consequently possesses no rights of self. Only as humble obedience is offered to Christ can one become this true "bond-servant."

There is a *fourth* lesson which I especially like. This duet teaches us that there is dignity in even the lowest task. One can be just a mere "messenger" and still be placed in an exalted position. In the church, there are various tasks begging for willing workers. It is not right for needed job to go unanswered because some feel it is "beneath their dignity."

Finally, we discover a *fifth* lesson in this duet. In the Savior's church there is an acceptance and love that is based upon the present "new man" and not upon the past "old man." It does not matter what you did years ago. When you demonstrate true obedience and repentance, you will find that "your past is not present with the Supreme Savior."

The second duet is composed of Luke and Demas (v. 14). These are two names that are familiar to the New Testament reader. Luke is mentioned by Paul as "the beloved physician." He was an intelligent and cultured man. He had joined Paul in Troas when the second missionary tour was in progress. He became a permanent traveling companion of the Apostle, accompanying him to Jerusalem, the imprisonment in Caesarea, and finally to Rome. So faithful was Luke to Paul that as the aged apostle wrote his last letter to Timothy he says, "*only Luke is with me*" (2 Timothy 4:11). The song of Luke echoes that of the first duet—fellowship in the Lord's church is great! Luke was concerned about the Colossians even though he had never met them.

The second member of this duet is Demas. We find three references to Demas in the New Testament (cf. Philemon 24; Colossians 4:14; 2 Timothy 4:10, 11). Some have arranged these three texts as an outline of apostasy. Although the texts do portray the correct pattern of apostasy, it is difficult to accept that the references in Philemon and Colossians were written to indicate Demas' apostasy. The letter to Philemon was written at the same time Colossians was; most likely all that separated their composition was a few days. It is hard to imagine that Demas' apostasy would have been noticed in such a short period of time. The song of Demas is that no matter how certain one may be about the Savior's supremacy, it can be misplaced! One should be careful that ardent zeal and enthusiasm for the Lord's church is not stifled by our love for the world.

IN THIS CHORUS WE DISCOVER...
ONE TRIO WHICH SINGS OF THE UNMATCHED DEVOTION WHICH IS GIVEN TO THE SAVIOR

The first member of this trio is Aristarchus (cf. Acts 19:29; 20:4; 27:2). From the Scriptures we are able to learn that he was a Macedonian from Thessalonica. He was unfortunate to have been dragged into the Ephesian theatre with Gaius during the riot instigated by the silversmiths. He sailed with Paul to Rome and suffered the shipwreck of that journey. Here we find a man who suffered beatings, storms, riots, ocean voyages, shipwreck, and prison for the Supreme Savior.

The second member of this trio is John Mark (cf. Acts 12:12, 25; 13:5, 13; 15:37, 39; 2 Timothy 4:11; Philemon 24; 1 Peter 5:13). Here is another colorful character. His mother's house was a frequent gathering place for the early disciples, and it is possible that it was in her home that our Lord observed the Last Supper. Barnabas was his cousin and Peter is credited for converting him. John Mark had journeyed with Paul and Barnabas on the first missionary tour but deserted them at Perga. In later time, and most likely through the help of Barnabas, John Mark once again climbed to the point of devoted service. John Mark wrote the gospel narrative that bears his name and, as Paul later wrote, "*...Take Mark, and bring him with thee; for he is useful to me for ministering*" (2 Timothy 4:11). Once again, we are able to discover a believer who had a past not present because of the Savior's supremacy.

The third member of this trio is Jesus Justus. We are ignorant about this man except for the facts that are revealed to us in our present text.

This trio harmonizes to bring our attention to focus on the following points regarding devotion. They teach us that *devotion may flag and fail.* We may disappoint our family and friends. We may even turn our backs on the firm commitment which we have pledged to Christ. But our devotion can be rekindled so that we can become "useful" once again. All of us have been "John Mark;" we have all stumbled and fallen. But once we looked again to the supremacy of Christ, our zeal and devotion was rekindled.

This trio teaches us that *true devotion will result in faithfulness and consistency in facing trials.* Once we have established the devotion of this trio, we will be able to face storms, trials, shipwrecks and threats just as Aristarchus!

This trio teaches us that this *devotion to the Savior enables us to be warmly "received" by our brethren.* Devotion will strengthen the fellowship bond and will assure our acceptance.

Finally, this trio teaches us that *devotion to the Savior will cause us to be a "comfort" to others.* These three were the only Jews in Rome who would associate with the Apostle in chains (cf. Acts 28:30; Philippians 1:15, 16). These three brethren were a "soothing relief" to Paul.

IN THIS CHORUS WE DISCOVER...
THREE SOLOISTS WHO SING OF THE SERVICE WHICH THE SUPREME SAVIOR DESIRES

The first soloist is Epaphras (vs. 12, 13; 1:7, 8). We have already had the opportunity of introducing ourselves to this preacher. He was a "bond-servant" whose greatest service was praying. Here is a man who was convinced of the Savior's ability to answer prayers. Paul tells us that Epaphras was one "striving" in his prayers. He put energy and effort into them. The NASV read that he was "laboring earnestly." Epaphras was careful to pray for ALL believers (v. 13). He prayed for the Colossians, Laodiceans, and those in Hierapolis. If he prayed for these brethren, we can be sure that his scope of concern was worldwide. Epaphras sings that service rendered for the Savior must be based upon a dedicated prayer life.

The second soloist is Nymphas (v. 15). There is some question as to whether this refers to a male or female household head. We choose to look at is as referring to a masculine figure. He and his household sing about one of the greatest services offered to the Supreme Savior—the Savior can be served by the whole family! The church met in his home and because of that, I am sure his family was strengthened. How wonderful it is for a family to be remembered as having the church assemble in their home.

The third soloist is Archippus (v. 17). His song centers on the duty of serving the Supreme Savior. As Paul addresses this gospel preacher, he encourages not to neglect his duty but make sure that they are filled full (cf. 1 Timothy 4:15; 2 Timothy 4:5). We must accept our duty and perform it even in difficult times because we are laboring "in the Lord."

DRAWING IT ALL TOGETHER

After we have examined this closing paragraph, how do you view it? Does it still look like a list of odd folks? Doesn't it carry a greater meaning and value to you?

What a grand conclusion to a grand letter. As you draw these characters together, you will discover the following exhortation:

Like Tychicus, we should be a beloved brother, faithful servant, and fellow bondslave in the Lord.

Like Aristarchus, John Mark, and Jesus Justus, we will prove to be an encouragement to others.

Like Epaphras, we will see the blessing of prayer and labor earnestly in prayer for our brethren.

Like the brethren of Laodicea, Colossae, and Hierapolis, we will "read" God's Word.

As Paul closes this letter, he stresses two things: *First*, he wanted the readers to "remember" his bonds. How passionate these words are! Because of the Savior, their beloved brother is sitting in a Roman jail. *Second*, he wanted to encourage them to "read." They needed to read diligently the inspired Scriptures. They should show an eagerness to receive and read all of the inspired writings available. Only through reading would they arrive at a full assurance of the Savior's greatness.

As the Apostle John looked into the majestic vision of heaven's glory, he witnessed a great chorus standing on the crystal sea (cf. Revelation 15:2-4). The amazing point to contemplate is that the song which the heavenly multitude sings in heaven is basically the same song that this chorus in Colossians 4 sings. The universal song which echoes in the hearts of all believers, whether they be in heaven or sojourners on earth, is clearly stated in the Book of Colossians—Jesus Christ is supreme! He alone is perfect! In Him only can man become complete!" Such is similar to the hymn we often sing, "Jesus is all the world to me, my life, my joy, MY ALL."

REFLECTIONS & RESOLUTIONS

Reflections from our study of Colossians 4:7-18:

1. Reflect on the characters listed in the lesson text. Which one seems to demonstrate the Savior's supremacy the most?

2. Reflect on how the Savior's supremacy changed the past of John Mark and Onesimus. Why is this a comforting thought? Do you think members of the church realize the great changes that the Savior has made in their lives? Have you ever known of someone who thought he just could never change some habit of life and become pleasing to God?

3. Reflect on the fellowship bond that is present in the church. How does the Savior help to establish this bond? Look back through Colossians and write down the references which stress the fellowship bond.

4. Reflect on the pattern of apostasy that Demas presents to us. Is this pattern true to reality? Why do you think the world has such an attraction to Christians? List some subtle ways, or allurements, used by the world to pull believers back from God.

Resolutions arising from our study of Colossians 4:7-18:

1. Resolve that you will be among that great chorus in heaven that sings of the Savior's supremacy.

2. Resolve that you will be a comfort and encouragement to others.

3. Resolve that, if you have become slack in your devotion like John Mark, you will rekindle zeal in your devotion quickly.

4. Resolve that you will see the greatness of the church, the seriousness of service, and the duty of devotion that is stressed in our lesson passage.

═ 16 ═

SHORT SKETCHES ON COLOSSIANS

These sketches of sermon outlines were developed in private study of the book of Colossians. With little study and preparation, they will be useful for lessons from the book of Colossians dealing with a them that is different from that of this present series. The sketches marked with (*) are outlines used in the present series and are fully developed in this book. It is hoped that these sketches will prove valuable to preachers, Bible class teachers, and others who are interested in gleaning precious lessons from this marvelous book.

1:1-2   **"Realizations in a Life Controlled by Christ's Supremacy!"** *

      a. Realize the wonderful providence of Almighty God – "will of God"
      b. Realize the beautiful tie that binds believers – "brethren in Christ"
      c. Realize the far surpassing blessings of God – "grace and peace"

	d. Realize the warm, filial relationship – "brother," "father"
1: 1-2	**"Important Associations in the Church"**

a. Apostle
b. Saints
c. Faithful brethren, brother
d. God, our Father

| 1:1-2 | **"Significant Characters in Colossians"** |

a. Paul the Apostle
b. Timothy, our brother
c. Members at Colossae, saints and brethren
d. Jesus, the Christ, Head, Lord, Master
e. "God, our Father"

| 1:1-2 | **"God Our Father" – What a Beautiful Thought** |

a. As our Father, we can lean upon Him for guidance and direction – "by the will of God"
b. As our Father, He seeks to give us the very best He possesses – "Grace and peace"
c. As our Father, we share in His character and actions – "saints"
d. As our Father, He binds all together in a wonderful family – "brethren"

| 1:1-2 | **"What All is Found 'in Christ'?"** |

a. Saints and fellow brethren
b. Grace and Peace
c. God, as our Father

| 1:3-8 | **"Epaphras: A Man with a Supreme Savior"** * |

a. A look at the life's work of this man (vs. 3-6)
b. A look at the virtues which helped this man do his work:
 1) Beloved (v. 7)
 2) Fellow bond-servant (v. 7)

        3) Faithful bond-servant of Christ (v. 7)
        4) He loved to talk about others (v. 8)
        5) He labored earnestly in prayers (4:12)

1:5b-7   **"The Blessed Gospel"**

    a. Its universal presence – "has come"
    b. Its universal scope – "all the world"
    c. Its simple reception – "heard," "understood," "learned"
    d. Its beautiful results – "bearing fruit and increasing"

1:3-8   **"Obligations to the Gospel"**

    a. It must be heard (v. 5)
    b. It must bear fruit (v. 6)
    c. It must be understood (v. 6b)
    d. It must be learned (v. 7)
    e. It has obligations because the gospel is the "Word of Truth," and it reveals the "grace of God in truth" (vs. 5b, 6b).

1:3-5   **"What is the Best News You Can Hear?"**

    a. News of one's faith in Christ
    b. News of one's accepting love
    c. News of one's eternal hope

1:3   **"Points for Profitable Prayer"**

    a. The ATTITUDE – "give thanks"
    b. The SCHEDULE – "praying always"
    c. The OBJECTS – "for you"
    d. The CONNECTION – "Lord, Jesus Christ (cf. 3:17)

1:4-5   **"Three Essential for Life" (cf. 1 Corinthians 13:13; 1 Thessalonians 1:2, 3)**

    a. FAITH in Jesus Christ
    b. LOVE demonstrated to all saints

        c. HOPE of the glories of heaven

1:9-14   **"Necessary Elements in our Salvation"**

        a. Our brethren – they must constantly pray for us (v. 9)
        b. Our personal commitment – we must decide and do (vs. 10-12a)
        c. Our blessed Father – He has qualified, delivered, and transferred (vs. 12b, 13a)
        d. Our loving Savior – He established the Kingdom, redeemed us, and provided forgiveness (vs. 13b, 14)

1:12-13   **"Great Thanksgiving"**

        a. He qualified us (v. 12)
        b. He delivered us (v. 13a)
        c. He transferred us (v. 13b)

1:9-14   **"What Will Happen When the Savior is Supreme in our Life?"** *

        a. There will be steadfast devotion and concern for others (v. 9).
        b. Constant mention in our prayers
        c. Sincere desire for advancement
        d. Desire that brethren will place Gods will foremost in their lives
        e. There will be a supreme desire to serve God in Life (vs. 10, 11).
        f. Walking in a worthy manner (v. 10a)
        g. Pleasing God in ALL respects (vs. 10b, 11)
        h. There will be an abounding in thanksgiving to God for all He has done (vs. 12, 13).
        i. He qualified us
        j. He delivered us
        k. He transferred us
        l. There will be a deep appreciation of Christ' sacrifice (vs. 13b, 14).

        m. He is the "beloved Son"!
        n. "In Him" there is redemption and forgiveness

1:9   **"The Beauty of Christian Brotherhood"**

        a. "Heard" – reception of news and update sought
        b. "Not cease to pray" – tender petitions for each other
        c. "May be filled" – gracious longing for each other's spiritual advancement

1:10-12   **"How to be Pleasing to God"**

        a. The ACTIONS necessary – bearing fruit, increasing in knowledge, strengthened in prayer
        b. The ATTITUDES necessary – giving thanks
        c. The ATTENTION necessary – in all respects
        d. The ATTAINMENTS necessary – steadfastness, patience, joy

1:10-12   **"What is the Acceptable Life?"**

        a. One that pleases God in ALL respects.
        b. One that bears fruit in EVERY good work.
        c. One that increases in knowledge of God.
        d. One that leans upon God for strength.
        e. One that expresses Christian virtues (patience, steadfastness, joy, and thanksgiving.

1:9-14   **"An Excellent Prayer Pattern"**

        a. As we offer prayers to God for our brethren's sake, we need to following this inspired pattern . . .
        b. It was offered constantly (v. 9a).

        c. It was offered asking for spiritual growth (v. 9b).
        d. It was offered asking for proper living (vs. 10, 11).
        e. It was offered asking that they would appreciate God's greatness (vs. 12-14).

1:9-14   "What Governs the Devoted Life?"

        a. Spiritual maturity (v. 9)
        b. Consecrated living (vs. 10, 11)
        c. Expressed thanksgiving (vs. 12, 13)

1:11b   "Three Results of Godly Living"

Living by the standards found in v. 10, 11a will cause the following results. There can be NO WAY to find these except by following verses 10, 11a.

        a. *Great endurance* in the face of temptation
        b. *Envious patience* in the face of trials
        c. *Joyful thanksgiving* to Almighty God for His wonderful blessing

1:12-13   "Salvation's Three Giant Steps"

        a. We are QUALIFIED – set apart from others
        b. We are DELIVERED – snatched from the captivity of Satan's snares
        c. We are TRANSFERRED – brought or placed "into" the Kingdom (body, or church) of His Son

Note: These are accomplished only when we hear, believe, confess, repent, and are immersed for forgiveness of sins.

1:9-14   "The Importance of Bible Study"

        a. Study is the foremost point in this prayer (v. 9a).

  b. Study is the only way to come to knowledge, wisdom and understanding (v. 9b).
  c. Study is the only way to "grow in knowledge" so that we can please God, live a worthy life, and be strengthened (vs. 10-11).
  d. Study is the only key to our being qualified, delivered, and transferred into God's Kingdom (vs. 12-14).

1:15-23 "The Savior's Supremacy" *

  a. Why is Christ the Supreme Savior? The text answers for us.
  b. Because of His deity (vs. 15, 19)
  c. Because of His awesome power (vs. 15b, 16, 17, 18b)
  d. Creation of all things
  e. Holds all things together
  f. Conquered death
  g. Because of His present position (v. 18a)
  h. Because of His ability to reconcile man with God (vs. 20-23)
  i. Because of God's desires (vs. 18c, 19a)

1:15-23 "Qualifications for the Savior's Supremacy"

  a. He is the image of God (vs. 15, 19)
  b. He is the supreme Creator (vs. 15b, 16)
  c. He is the supreme Controller (v. 17)
  d. He is the Head of the church (v. 18a)
  e. He is the supreme Conqueror of death (v. 18b)
  f. He is the only means of reconciliation to God (vs. 20-23)

1:19-23 "God's Wish for Humanity"

  a. For the fulness of deity to dwell in Christ
  b. For all men to have a way of reconciliation
  c. For all to find peace, holiness, blamelessness
  d. For all to "continue" after reconciliation

1:15-23   **"Evidences of Christ's Deity"**

       a.   He is the image of God.

       b.   His actions are those of a divine being with absolute power – creation, authority, control, conquering death and sin.

       c.   His pre-existence necessitates His deity.

1:22-23   **"Our Presentation Before God"**

       a.   To stand before God on the Judgment Day and hear Him extend to us the wonderful invitation to "enter in" to Heaven's splendor, must be preceded by two things which are done on earth.

       b.   We must be reconciled to God through Jesus Christ and thereby become holy, blameless, and beyond reproach.

       c.   We must be constant in our faith, firmly established, steadfast, and not moved away from our eternal hope.

1:15-23   **"Basic Elements of the Gospel"**

       a.   The wonderful gospel is explained in this text . . .

       b.   It contains vital face about Christ.

       c.   It contains vital exhortations for the child of God (vs. 21-23).

       d.   It must be published as far and as effectively as in Paul's time (v. 23b).

       e.   All of the Gospel must be accepted if we are to receive heaven's rewards.

1:20-23   **"The Conditional Nature of God's Plan"**

       a.   There is the "if" of one accepting the plan of reconciliation (vs. 20-22a).

b. There is the "if" of being presented to God in an acceptable position – holy blameless, beyond reproach (v. 22b).
c. There is the "if" of continuing in the faith, in the proper manner (v. 23).

1:21-23 **The "Before" and the "After"**

In the text, we are able to see a dramatic contrast between those living *without* Christ and those living life *with* Christ.

a. Consider the calamity BEFORE Christ (v. 21).
   1) Alienated from God
   2) Hostile toward God
   3) Thoughts were corrupt
   4) ALL behavior was active in evil.
b. Consider the beauty and blessing AFTER Christ (vs. 22, 23).
   1) Reconciled to God by Christ's sacrifice (v. 22a)
   2) New Attitudes – holy, blameless, beyond reproach (v. 22b)
   3) New determination – continue in faith (v. 223).
c. It is a grand thought that ALL men have the opportunity of living life being blessed by God because they are "in Christ."
d. "Formerly," "now," "hope," "peace"

1:21-23 **"Personal Duties"**

a. You must be reconciled to God (vs. 21, 22).
b. You must be presented to God (v. 22b).
c. You must "hear" the gospel (v. 23)
d. You must take the gospel to all creation (v. 23).

1:21-23 **"Consequential Actions"**

a. Having heard, we obeyed.

      b. Having obeyed, we were reconciled.
      c. Having been reconciled, we became ministers.
      d. Having become ministers, we will be properly presented to God.
      e. Having been properly presented, we will lay hold on the hope of the Gospel.

1:24-29   **"Attitudes of One Who Has a Supreme Savior"** *

      a. Rejoicing in all circumstances (v. 24).
      b. Willingness to accept responsibility— "do my share" (v. 24).
      c. Unselfishness (v. 24).
      d. Love and concern for brethren
      e. "For your benefit (v. 25)
      f. Teaching and wonderful mystery (v. 28)
      g. Striving for their growth (v. 29)
      h. Keep eyes on true values – "riches" (v. 27).
      i. A blessed trust in God's Providential will – "God willed" (v. 27); v. 29 Paul's power came from God.

1:24-29   **"Objectives of Paul that are Suitable to Us"**

      a. To do his share in the church and to complete the work (v. 24).
      b. To perform his duties as a minister and a steward (v. 25).
      c. To enlighten all men about God's glorious mystery (vs. 26, 27).
      d. To proclaim Jesus Christ to make all men complete [perfect] (vs. 28, 29).

1:24-29   **"Paul's Labors"**

      a. I rejoice (v. 24a).
      b. I do my share (v. 24b).
      c. I (we) proclaim fully (v. 28).
      d. I labor (v. 29).

1:28-29 "The Teacher of Christ"

 a. The teacher's duties (v. 28).
 b. Proclaim
 c. Admonish
 d. Teach
 e. The teacher's scope of duty – "every man" (v. 28).
 f. The teacher's attitude in his duty—
 g. Wisdom governs his teaching (v. 28)
 h. Striving describes his efforts (v 29)
 i. The teacher's supreme goal is to "present every man complete in Christ" (v. 28b).

1:24-29 "Teachings About Christ"

 a. His body (the church) fills all needs in life.
 b. Those possessing Christ have great riches—the hope of glory.
 c. Perfection in life is found only "in Christ."

1:24-29 "I Do My Share"

 a. Paul's use of this expression is to encourage further work, not to evade further duty!
 b. His share was always increasing. Paul never did all he could. His share was doing what needed to be done.
 c. His share was a stewardship given to him by God (v. 25).
 d. His share included looking for brethren's needs and fulfilling these needs. This attitude required:
 e. Humility – willingness to serve others.
 f. Willingness – to accept a God-give duty.
 g. Concern – for brethren (cf. v. 28b).
 h. Wisdom – to admonish properly.

        i. Paul did his share by trusting God for strength (v. 29).

1:24-29   **"God willed..."**

a. That through preaching Christ is known.
b. That only in Christ hope is found
c. That willing service should fill up what is lacking.
d. That true riches are only in Christ.
e. That every man be complete in Christ.
f. That those who labor for His cause should receive strength to continue.

1:28-29   **"Christian Duties"**

a. To proclaim Christ
b. To admonish every man.
c. To teach every man according to wisdom.
d. To present every man complete [perfect].
e. To labor and strive according to God's power.

1:24-29   **"What God Has Done"**

a. He has "bestowed" duties upon us (v. 25)
b. He has "willed" to make salvation known (v. 27)
c. He has provided "power" for us to do His will (v. 29).

2:1-5   **"A Supreme Savior Will Drastically Change You!"** *

a. It drastically changes the way you feel toward people (vs. 1, 4).
b. It drastically changes the way you view the church (vs. 2, 3).
c. It becomes a source of great encouragement.
d. It becomes a close-knit group of believers.
e. It becomes the means of providing complete understanding of God's will.

	f. It becomes the church universal instead of the church only local (v. 1b).
	g. It drastically changes your standard of joy (v. 5b).
2:1-5	"The Supreme Savior's Gifts"
	a. He gives love which is surpassed and is reflected in believer's lives (vs. 1, 2a).
	b. He gives riches and treasures which are incomparable with those of the world (vs. 2b, 3).
	c. He gives knowledge which enlightens rather than error which deludes (vs. 2c, 4).
	d. He gives us fellowship to transcend miles of separation, and true joy found in discipline and faith (v. 5).
2:1-5	"Struggling for Others"
	a. This struggle is all-encompassing – whether the believers are known or unknown (v. 1).
	b. This struggle will provide total encouragement (v. 2).
	c. Encourages hearts
	d. A close and binding love
	e. Full assurance of faith
	f. Riches of complete understanding
	g. This struggle counteracts deception (v. 4)
	h. This struggle transcends space and obstacles (v. 5a).
	i. This struggle results in a great "delight" (v. 5b).
2:2	"Treasures of Understanding"
	a. Hearts are encouraged
	b. Hearts are knit together
	c. Full assurance and understanding
	d. A true knowledge of God's mystery

2:2	**"Essential Factors for Encouragement"**

        a. A united love which knits members together
        b. Mature development into a full assurance of understanding.
        c. A grounded and TRUE knowledge of how Jesus Christ provides redemption for us.

2:1-5	**"What Invites Deception?"**

        a. Failure to communicate with brethren (vs. 1a, 4a).
        b. Failure to edify one another (v. 2).
        c. Failure to be grounded in the true knowledge of God's mystery (vs. 2b-4).
        d. Failure to be open with each other (vs 1, 4, 5). Paul was open enough to let these brethren know he struggled for them, and rejoiced over their good deeds and faith.

2:1-5	**"Long Distance Knitting"**

        a. Although separated by miles, Paul was careful to keep his fellowship bond strong. What effect did this long-distance knitting have?
        b. It further strengthened and established fellowship (v. 1).
        c. It provided opportunity for edification (v. 2).
        d. It provided opportunity for Bible study to be encouraged (vs. 2b, 3).
        e. It enabled Paul to exhort faithfulness (vs. 4, 5).

2:5	**"Two Things Which Always Cause Joy"**

        a. Good discipline
        b. Stability of faith

2:6-15	**"A Life Lived with the Supreme Savior"** *

        a. It is a life that begins with "receiving" Christ (vs. 6, 12).

	b. It is a life that is dedicated to Christ (v. 7).
	c. It is a life guarding against error (v. 8).
	d. It is a life of victory assured by Christ's supremacy (vs. 9-15).
2:15	**"The Completeness of Christ's Victory"**
	a. He disarmed the rulers.
	b. He made a public display of their failure.
	c. He triumphed over them.
2:9-15	**"A Testimony to Christ's Greatness"**
	a. In Him all the fulness of Deity dwells (v. 9).
	b. In Him we are made complete (v. 10)
	c. In Him universal authority resides (vs. 10b, 15).
	d. In Him spiritual union with God is found (vs. 11-14).
	e. True circumcision (v. 11).
	f. Spiritual resurrection through baptism (vs. 12, 13).
	g. The spiritual covenant is founded by His authority (v. 14).
2:6-7	**"How to Walk in Christ"**
	a. Be firmly rooted
	b. Be built up in Him
	c. Be established in your faith
	d. Be overflowing with gratitude
2:8	**"What Will Captivate Us in Error?"**
	a. Philosophy void of faith in God.
	b. Deception by "persuasive" speech (cf. v. 4).
	c. Trust and allegiance to man's traditions.
	d. Love and longing for the world.

2:8-10	**"A Vivid Contrast to Consider"**

    a. Some receive Christ while others receive the traditions of men (vs. 6, 8).
    b. Some find freedom in Christ while others remain captive of Satan (v. 8).
    c. Some find fullness and completeness in Jesus Christ while others are empty in empty deception (vs. 9, 10, 18).

2:9-12	**"Christ's Covenant is Greater than Moses'"**

    a. Its author is far greater (vs. 9, 10b).
    b. It affords completeness (v. 10)
    c. Its circumcision is more effective (v. 14).
    d. Its terms of admission are better (v. 12).

2:6-15	**"Blessings Found in Christ"**

    a. The blessings are listed:
    b. A rewarding lifestyle (vs. 6, 7).
    c. A complete and full life (v. 10).
    d. Spiritual circumcision (v. 11).
    e. Spiritual resurrection – forgiveness of sins (v. 13).
    f. Release from the law (v. 14).
    g. Complete triumph (v. 15).
    h. The way to share in these blessings stated:
    i. Through baptism (v. 12).
    j. By walking "in Him" (v. 6).

2:13	**"The Gentile's Salvation Discussed"**

    a. Their lost state: Because of sin and alien status "uncircumcised."
    b. Their saved state:
    c. Due to God's love – "He made"
    d. Due to their union with Christ – "with Him" (v. 12).

e. Due to God's mercy and pardon following obedience – "ALL" was forgiven.

2:16-23 **"Supplanting Christ's Supremacy!"** *

a. What things will supplant Christ's supremacy?
   1) Allegiance to the Old Testament (vs. 16, 17).
   2) False humility (v. 18a).
   3) Worship of angels (v. 18b).
   4) Visions (v. 18c).
b. Why are these improper substitutes for Christ?
   1) They are based upon man, not God (vs. 16, 18).
   2) They are not the true "substance."
   3) They fail to give the proper dues to the "head (v. 19).
c. What will be the consequences of following these things?
   1) We will live as if we were still in the world (v. 20).
   2) We will worship by "self-made" rules (v. 23).
   3) We will submit to foolish commands (v. 21).
   4) We will trust on things that are worldly (vs. 22, 23).
   5) We will be "robbed" of our prize (v. 18).
d. How does Christ's supremacy affect our views of these supplanters? (vs. 19, 20).

2:16-23 **"Why is Jesus Christ Supreme?"**

a. Because He is the substance (vs. 16, 17).
b. Because He is the head (vs. 18, 19).
c. Because He gives freedom for living (vs. 20-23).

2:20-23 "What Your New Relationship with Christ Means"

    a. You have died WITH Christ (v. 20a).
    b. You are no longer living by the world's principles (v. 20b).
    c. You are not to submit to man's decrees (vs. 20c-22).
    d. You are now following true values (v. 23).

2:16-19 "Grounds for Disqualifications"

    a. False humility (v. 18a).
    b. False worship (v. 18b).
    c. False spirituality (v. 18c).
    d. False authority (v. 19).

2:16-23 "Consequences of Following Man's Teachings"

    a. Unequal, outdated, and inconsistent judging (v. 16).
    b. Rejection of Christ as authority in religion (vs. 17, 19, 20).
    c. Disqualification from the prize (v. 18).
    d. Growth that is NOT from God (v. 19b).
    e. Useless value system (v. 23b).
    f. Everything founded upon man's doctrine is destined "to perish!" (v. 22).

2:16-23 "The Problems of Many Religions Today"

    a. The present religious world suffers today because...
        1) There are those who are too restrictive – they bind observance of days, diets, etc.
        2) There are those who look to spiritual beings rather than to God – dead saints, angels, etc.
        3) There are those who cannot break with the world's principles.

- b. Because of these problems, the following arise...
  1) Disqualification
  2) Minds are puffed up with idle notions
  3) Connection with God is severed
  4) Inability to cope with the world's allurements
  5) Eventual death
- c. What will change these results and remedy the problems? A correct view of Christ Jesus!
  1) As the reality of God's promises
  2) As the head (authority) of God's covenant
  3) As the way to freedom in living life

2:16-23 **"Which Commands Must I Follow?**

There are two basic standards by which we are to be directed in religion. Paul is careful to examine each and then how us which one we must follow.

- a. There is the standard of man's judgment.
  1) It is only a shadow.
  2) It delights in outward demonstration.
  3) It rests upon subjective standards.
  4) It has no connection with God – thus no value.
  5) Its future is dismal – destined to perish.
- b. There is the standard of God's Judgment
  1) Here is reality!
  2) Here is an intimate connection, hence supreme value.
  3) It is destined for heavenly splendor because it is based upon God.
- c. The conclusion: Do not allow just anyone to judge, but allow God, the righteous Judge, to decide what actions are proper in your life. By this choice you will be supported and held up and will grow as God desired!

2:19   **"A Dead Connection"**

    a. What cause this "lost connection?"
        1) Following men and not God
        2) Observing the shadow and not the reality.
        3) Rejection of God's standards for self.
    b. What results from "lost connection?"
        1) Disqualification from the prize
        2) Errors in worship
        3) Mind becomes puffed up with idle notions
        4) Improper growth
    c. What will restore this "lost connection?"
        1) Realization that you have died with Christ.
        2) Acceptance of knowledge of the freedom in Christ Jesus.
        3) Rejection of the world's principles.
    d. What will happen if this "lost connection" is not restored? "Perish!" (v. 22).

2:20   **"Dying with Christ"**

What all results whenever we die "with" Christ?

    a. We are freed from the petty judgments of men.
    b. We are able to grasp the reality found in Christ.
    c. We are qualified for the prize.
    d. We become part of the body which grows as God desires.
    e. We are freed from the world's principles.

2:17   **"FOR REAL!"**

Paul assures us that "the reality is found in Christ" (v. 17) Note the following things that become a reality with Jesus Christ.

    a. Salvation from sins is real (Hebrews 9:13, 14; 10:1-4).

b. Membership in God's Kingdom is real.
c. Freedom is real.
1) Freedom to live life to its fullest (Romans 6:17, 18).
2) Freedom to serve and worship God according to spirit, not law (Romans 7:6).
3) Freedom from the oppressive and restrictive opinions of man (v. 16).
d. Access to all spiritual blessings and a source of power that is able to do more than we ever imagined is for real (Ephesians 1:3; 3:20).

What a grand thought this is! The reality IS found in Jesus Christ.

3:1-4 **"Followers of the Supreme Savior are Marked!"** *

Those who own Jesus Christ as their Savior will have certain behavior mannerisms which are unmistakable and will cause them to be marked as His followers:

a. They have been raised with Christ (vs. 1a, 3a).
b. They keep seeking the things above (v. 1b).
c. They have a spiritual mindset (v 2).
d. They live with assurances of promises being fulfilled (v. 4).
e. They enjoy a secure mind (v. 3b).

3:1-4 **"Consequences of Obedience"**

In this text, Paul lists the consequences which follow obedience – If then...

a. Keep seeking the things above (v. 1).
b. You will be intent on spiritual matters (v. 2).
c. Your spiritual life is secured by God (v. 3).
d. You will rest in anticipation of Christ's coming (v. 4).

3:1-4 **"Why Should Christians be Different?"**

    a. Because we have died and have risen with Christ (vs. 1, 3a).
    b. Because we are seeking the things above (v. 1b).
    c. Because we think on spiritual things, not earthly (v. 2).
    d. Because we want spiritual security (v. 3b)
    e. Because our life is Christ, not the world (v. 4a).
    f. Because we want to be revealed *with* Him in glory (v 4).

3:1-3 **"ABOVE"**

In verses 1-3, we see that Paul repeats the word "above" as referring to the believer's life. Consider the emphasis this has on the Christian.

    a. The Christian's AMBITION is "above" – "keep seeking."
    b. The Christian's SAVIOR is enthroned "above"— "at right hand."
    c. The Christian's AFFECTIONS are "above" – "set your hearts."
    d. The Christian's SECURITY is "above" – "hid with Christ"

3:1-4 **"The Mindset of the Christian"**

Paul commands us to "set our mind" (cf. Philippians 4:8, 9).

    a. Its BEGINNING – being raised with Christ.
    b. Its OBJECTIVE – seeking the things above.
    c. Its GREATEST ENEMY – things upon the earth.
    d. Its REWARD – revealed with Christ in glory.
    e. Its ALL-IMPORTANT REASON – Christ is our life!

3:5-11 "The Past IS NOT Present with the Savior" *

a. A sober look at the PAST.
b. A relieved look at how the past was changed by Christ.
c. A thankful look at the PRESENT.

3:5-11 "Walking with the Supreme Savior"

Begin by discussing the word "walk" and its application in Scripture. What is this "walk" like?

a. It puts to death worldly passions (vs. 5, 6).
b. It makes a clear and uncompromising distance between the world and the spiritual (vs. 7, 8a).
c. It demonstrates self-control (v. 8b).
d. It enhances ALL relationships (vs. 9-11).
   1) With one another (vs. 9a, 11a).
   2) With one's self – "since you" (v. 9b). From the old to the new.
   3) With God (vs. 10, 11b).

3:5-11 "Death and Life"

The Christian has the duty to "die" and to "live."

a. To what must the Christian die?
   1) All aspects of sin in our bodies (vs. 5, 7).
   2) All kinds of sins of the tongue (vs. 8, 9a).
   3) All evil practices (v. 9b).
b. To what is the Christian to live?
   1) A renewal in heart and hand which mirrors God (v. 10).
   2) A renewal of the universal brotherhood of believers (v. 11a).
   3) A renewal of the Supremacy of Christ in life (v. 11b).
c. Why must we die to the world and live until Jesus Christ? (v. 6). "For the wrath of God will come!"

3:7   **"The Way They Were"**

One of the most delightful experiences in life is to run into someone whose life has undergone a fantastic change for the better because of Christ's influence. Such is the case in this text.

- a. We see the way they used to be...
  1) They were fully devoted to passions (v. 5).
  2) They were vulgar, and vain in speech (v. 8).
  3) They were unconcerned for fellow men (v. 9).
- b. We see the way they are now...
  1) Everything contrary to God was removed (v. 8a).
  2) They have a mutual concern because of unity in Christ (v. 11).
- c. How did this change take place?
  1) They "put to death."
  2) They "put off."
  3) They "put on."
  4) They were "renewed."
  5) They looked seriously at the "wrath of God."

3:5-11   **"The Wrath of God"**

- a. It is spoken of as a certain thing – "will come."
- b. It will come because of sin – "on account of those things."
- c. It can be avoided – "put aside and put on the new."

3:5-11   **"Factors Which Help to Ease Prejudice"**

- a. A renewal of the knowledge of God's love (vs. 10a 11).
- b. A determined effort to exercise self-control (v. 9b).

c. Putting to death sin in our lives (v. 5).
d. Proper speech (vs. 8, 9a).
e. Maturing into the image of God who created Christ (v. 10b).
f. Realizing the penalty for those who foster prejudice in their hearts (v. 6b) – "the wrath of God." (cf. James 2:8, 9; Malachi 2:9b; 3:5).

3:8-9 **"A Critical Tongue"**

What all does Paul have to say about the person who does not govern his tongue in the proper way?

a. He has neglected to put off the old man.
b. He is unable to put on the new man.
c. He fails to possess true knowledge which renews the soul.
d. His life is devoted to "evil practices."
e. His future – "the wrath of God will come!"

3:5-11 **"The Old and the New" (cf. Ephesians 4:17-32)**

a. A general discussion of the old man (vs. 5-9).
b. A general discussion of the new man (vs. 10-11).
c. A discussion of what makes the difference.
d. Knowledge which comes from God (v. 10).
e. Actions in response to knowledge (1 Corinthians 6:9-11; Colossians 3:9).
f. Dedication to obeying God's will in life following our actions (vs. 7b, 8a; v. 10 "being renewed")

3:12-17 **"Supremacy Visibility!"** *

a. By living a life distinctive (vs. 12a, 17).
   1) Chosen by God
   2) Holy in practice

          3) Dearly loved of God
          4) Devoted to God (v. 17)
     b. By clothing yourself with godly apparel (vs. 12b-15).
          1) Compassion
          2) Kindness
          3) Humility
          4) Meekness
          5) Longsuffering
          6) Forbearing
          7) Forgiving
          8) Love
          9) Unity of the body
     c. By possessing the reality of salvation (vs. 15, 16).
          1) Peace
          2) Thanksgiving
          3) Teaching and admonishing

3:12-17 **"The Way to Unity in the Church"**

     a. Allow the proper HEART to direct your associations in the body (vs. 12-15).
     b. Allow the proper STANDARD to direct your teachings (v. 16).
     c. Allow the proper AUTHORITY to direct your whole life (v. 17).

3:13 **"Forgiveness"**

     a. The command is given.
     b. The standard is given – "as the Lord forgave."
     c. The reasons are given.
     d. Because the Lord did so.
     e. Because love demands it.
     f. Because unity and harmony depend upon it.
     g. The subjects of the command are given – "chosen," "beloved of God."

        h. The attitudes necessary to accomplish are described – compassion, kindness, gentleness, patience.

3:12   **"Forbearing"**

        a. Its SCOPE – personal complaints (v. 13)
        b. Its BASIS – a character molded after God (vs. 12, 13).
        c. Its NECESSITY – because we are God's elect and beloved.
        d. Its DURATION –as long and as oft as the Lord (v. 13b).
        e. Its RESULT . . .
            1) The peace of Christ rules the heart (v. 15).
            2) Perfectness (v. 14b).
            3) Thanksgiving (vs. 15b, 16b, 17b).
        f. Its MOTIVATION – love (v. 14b).

3:12-17   **"The Unique Readers of Colossians"**

        a. They were "chosen" of God (v. 12).
        b. They have been "forgiven" of the Lord (v. 13).
        c. They were "called" of God (v. 15).
        d. They are "thankful" to God (vs. 16, 17).

3:12-17   **"Those Who are Chosen of God"**

        a. They demonstrate a specific lifestyle— "holy."
        b. They occupy a special place in God's heart – "beloved."
        c. They demonstrate special actions toward others – "compassion," "kindness" "humility," "gentleness," "patience," "forbearance," "forgiveness," "teaching," "admonishing," "love."
        d. They possess the "peace of Christ."
        e. They are "thankful."

3:12-17   **"Filling the Void"**

Void will [must] be filled! Paul has commanded us to "put off" (3:5-11), now he commands us to fill the void.

    a. Fill it with knowledge of your relationship with God – "chosen," "beloved" (v. 12a).
    b. Fill it with a transformed life toward others (vs. 12b, 13).
    c. Fill it with unity (vs. 14, 15).
    d. Fill it with the "word of Christ" (vs. 16, 17a.
    e. Fill it with thanksgiving (vs. 15b, 16b, 17b).

3:25   **"The Judgment of God"**

    a. The wrong-doer will certainly stand in judgment!
    b. The wrong-doer will certainly pay the consequences of his sin!
    c. The wrong-doer will be judged in a personal way – "he has done!"
    d. The wrong-doer will be judged impartially!

3:18–4:1   **"The Leaven of Christ's Supremacy"** *

    a. It touches the life of the wife (3:18).
    b. It touches the life of the husband (3:19).
    c. It touches the life of the children (3:20).
    d. It touches the lives of the parents (3:21).
    e. It touches the life of the employee (3:22-25).
    f. It touches the life of the employer (3:25; 4:1).

3:18-21   **"Family Matters"**

    a. For the wives (v. 18)
        1) Be submissive.
        2) Live as fitting God's will.
    b. For the husbands (v. 19).
        1) Love your wives.
        2) Treat wives properly.

  c. For the children (v. 20).
    1) Obey in ALL things
    2) Be well-pleasing to Christ.
  d. For the parents (v. 21).
    1) Discipline in the proper manner.
    2) See that the child is brought up with a well-founded development – spiritually, emotionally, mentally, and socially.

3:22–4:1 **"The Christian's Work Ethic"**

  a. The ethics of labor (3:22-24)
    1) The SCOPE of this ethical standard – "all things."
    2) The OBLIGATION of this ethical standard – "obey."
    3) The EMOTIONS of this ethical standard -- "sincerity," "fearing," "heartily."
    4) The REASON for this ethical standard – "ye serve the Lord!"
  b. The ethics of management (4:1).
    1) The ACTIONS which should characterize them – "justice," "fairness."
    2) The REALIZATION which should guide them – they serve a great Master in heaven.
  c. Divine work ethics will be the standard for all to be judged (3:25).

3:23 **"Hearty Work"**

  a. Mothers and wives work heartily for the Lord (3:18, 21).
  b. Fathers and husbands work heartily for the Lord (3:19, 21).
  c. Employees and employers work heartily for the Lord (3:21 – 4:1).
  d. Sons and daughters work heartily for the Lord (3:2).

4:2-6   **"Hankerings Fostered by the Savior's Supremacy"** *

    a. A longing for others to know the joy of prayer (v. 2).
    b. A longing for constant opportunities to teach the gospel of Christ (vs. 3, 4).
    c. A longing for fellow brethren to live exemplary lives (vs. 5, 6).
       1) Conduct guided by wisdom.
       2) Grasping every opportunity to spread the truth.
       3) Seasoned speech in their answers.

4:2-4   **"Duties in Prayer"**

    a. Duties of a personal nature (v. 2).
       1) Devote yourself – continue steadfastly.
       2) Keep alert – be watchful.
       3) Be thankful.
    b. Duties of our prayers for brethren (vs. 3, 4).
       1) Pray for others (v. 3a).
       2) Pray for opportunities (v. 3b).
       3) Pray for others as they speak and teach the gospel (v. 4).

4:2-6   **"Personal Commands from Paul"**

    a. Devote yourself to prayer (v. 2-4).
    b. Conduct yourself wisely (v. 5a).
    c. Take advantage of opportunities (v. 5b).
    d. Be sure to speak properly (v. 6a).
    e. Be sure to "answer" each unbeliever (v. 6b).

4:2-6   **"Wonderful Uses of your Tongue"**

    a. Use it in devoted prayer (vs. 2, 3a).
    b. Use it to speak God's Word clearly (v. 3b, 4).
    c. Use it to season lives of unbelievers with grace (v. 5, 6).

4:2-6   "**Guidelines for Living with Non-Believers**"

         a.   Be devoted in prayer for strength to live with unbelievers properly (vs. 2, 3).
         b.   Be alert to all opportunities of teaching (v. 3).
         c.   Be simple in talking about salvation (v. 4).
         d.   Be wise in using your time with the unbeliever (v. 5).
         e.   Be seasoned in your speech (v. 6).

4:2-6   "**Preaching the Word of God**"

         a.   Preaching is assisted by praying (vs. 2, 3a).
         b.   Preaching is taking advantage of the "door" for the word (v. 3b).
         c.   Preaching is to make known the mystery of Christ (vs. 3c, 4).
         d.   Preaching must be with "seasoned speech" (vs. 5, 6).

4:6   "**Christian Conversation is a Great Blessing**"

         a.   It is always full of grace.
         b.   It is "seasoned with salt."
         c.   It is capable of giving a proper answer to everybody!

4:7-18   "**A Chorus Sings Christ's Supremacy!**" *

The lives of these sainted believers present a triumphant son of the majesty and supremacy of Jesus Christ. Note the effects of the Supreme Savior controlling their wills.

         a.   There are two DUETS in this chorus –
              1)   Tychicus and Onesimus (vs. 7-9).
              2)   Luke and Demas (vs. 8, 9).
         b.   There is one TRIO in this chorus – Aristarchus, John Mark, and Jesus Justus (vs. 10, 11).
         c.   There are two SOLOISTS in this chorus –
              1)   Epaphras (vs. 12, 13; 1:7, 8).

2) Archippus (v. 17).

4:7-18 **"Some Blessings Which Christian Friends Yield"**

a. Joint labor in spreading the gospel (vs. 7, 9, 11).
b. Encouraged hearts (vs. 8b, 11).
c. Uplifting news and information (v. 9b).
d. Careful concern about spiritual matters (vs. 12, 13, 18).
e. Earnest prayers (v. 12).
f. Exhortation to serve Christ (v. 17).

4:7-18 **"Exhortation from a Prison Cell"**

a. Welcome fellow brethren who travel to you (v. 10).
b. Greet fellow brethren who live around you (v. 15).
c. Read the holy Scriptures (v. 16). Take heed to our labors for the Lord and fulfill them (v. 17).
d. Remember! (v. 18).

4:12-13 **"Edification According to Epaphras"**

a. THE REASON –
   1) You are members together.
   2) You are "bondslaves" of Jesus Christ.
   3) You should share a deep concern.
b. THE ATTITUDE – "laboring earnest for you."
c. THE OBJECTIVE – stand perfect and fully assured in all the will of God.
d. THE SCOPE – toward ALL brethren!

4:17-18 **"How Will We Behave if Christ is Supreme in Our Lives?"**

a. Like Tychicus, we will be a beloved brother, faithful servant, and fellow bondslave in the Lord (v. 7).

b. Like Aristarchus, Mark, and Justus, we will prove to be an encouragement (v. 11).
c. Like Epaphras, we will see the necessity of prayer (v. 12a).
d. Like Epaphras, we will labor earnestly to help our fellow brethren mature (v. 12b).
e. Like the Colossians, we will "remember" (v. 18).
f. Like the brethren at Colossae, Laodicea, and Hierapolis, we will read God's Word (v. 16).

Made in the USA
Columbia, SC
22 March 2022